Purposeful
Co-Teaching

Real Cases and Effective Strategies

**Greg
Conderman** **Val
Bresnahan** **Theresa
Pedersen**

CORWIN PRESS
A SAGE Company

For information:

Corwin Press
A SAGE Company
2455 Teller Road
Thousand Oaks, California 91320
www.corwinpress.com

SAGE Ltd.
1 Oliver's Yard
55 City Road
London EC1Y 1SP
United Kingdom

SAGE India Pvt. Ltd.
B 1/I 1 Mohan Cooperative
    Industrial Area
Mathura Road, New Delhi 110 044
India

SAGE Asia-Pacific Pte. Ltd.
33 Pekin Street #02-01
Far East Square
Singapore 048763

Printed in the United States of America.

Library of Congress Cataloging-in-Publication Data

Conderman, Greg.
Purposeful co-teaching: real cases and effective strategies/Greg Conderman,
Val Bresnahan, Theresa Pedersen.
    p. cm.
Includes bibliographical references and index.
ISBN 978-1-4129-6448-7 (cloth)
ISBN 978-1-4129-6449-4 (pbk.)
    1. Teaching teams. 2. Individualized instruction. 3. Education, Elementary.
4. Education, Secondary. I. Bresnahan, Val. II. Pedersen, Theresa. III. Title.

LB1029.T4C66 2009
371.1'48—dc22   2008021947

This book is printed on acid-free paper.

08   09   10   11   12   10   9   8   7   6   5   4   3   2   1

Acquisitions Editor:	David Chao
Editorial Assistant:	Mary Dang
Production Editor:	Libby Larson
Copy Editor:	Paula L. Fleming
Typesetter:	C&M Digitals (P) Ltd.
Proofreader:	Wendy Jo Dymond
Indexer:	Ellen Slavitz
Cover Designer:	Lisa Riley

Contents

Preface

Enter your classroom of 28 students. Six students have individualized education plans (IEPs), one is autistic, three have limited English skills, and an additional four live in the subsidized housing apartment complex on the community's outskirts. Three students just moved into the district, while six have lived here since kindergarten. One student received services through the gifted program but was recently reassigned to your classroom. Seven students did not meet standards on the state assessment test, while five exceeded standards. Several students in your class are experiencing serious issues, such as divorce, loss of a home, blended families, abuse, abandonment, and other emotional challenges, which seriously impact their behavior, attentiveness, and learning.

While this may sound like a fictitious classroom proposed for the purpose of this book, this classroom really exists, as do many others like it across the country. This example is not from a school in an inner-city urban area but rather a classroom in an upper-middle-class suburban school district. This is not a special education classroom but rather a general education classroom taught by a general education language arts teacher. This teacher may be you, and your assignment is to teach them all—to leave none behind.

Ensuring the success of each student, regardless of ethnicity, background, gender, skills, emotional status, or income level, embodies the mandate of the 2002 legislation No Child Left Behind (NCLB). Fulfilling this mandate by helping each child learn in large classrooms represents a tremendous challenge for teachers—quite a different task from that faced by our predecessors in classrooms at the turn of the previous century. The public school classroom of the early 1900s was the vehicle to homogenize immigrants coming to America. The theme of the factory model of education was "One size fits all." In contrast, teachers of the twenty-first century have been mandated to ensure success for each student. This necessitates a change in emphasis from teaching *all* to teaching *each*. But how can one teacher meet the needs of such a diverse student body? The answer may be found in co-teaching.

Co-teaching occurs when two or more professionals jointly deliver substantive instruction to a diverse, blended group of students in a single physical space (Friend & Cook, 2007). On the surface, co-teaching may merely appear to be two teachers in the same classroom. However, to understand and benefit from co-teaching, a paradigm shift is needed—think of the experience of 3-D image viewing.

Have you ever been challenged with a "magic eye" picture? This picture includes an image on the surface that is readily apparent, but underneath that image is another, a three-dimensional picture, which will emerge only if you change your perspective. Some easily change their perspective and see the 3-D image immediately. Others need coaching, specific directions, and lots of practice. With persistence and many trials, however, the image eventually emerges.

Co-teaching also requires a shift in perspective, but this shift is a change in perspective about how you view yourself, your class, and your teaching. As you change your perspective, from a single teacher delivering the curriculum to an entire class to a co-teacher working collaboratively to meet the individual needs of *each* student, you will begin to experience the rewards of co-teaching. For some, this perspective switch happens within the first few weeks; for others, it may take months or even an entire school year; and for some, the image never emerges.

To see the 3-D image emerge in the "magic eye" picture, the trick is to keep your eye on a distant target. Co-teaching is like this, also. Keep your eye on the target—the individual learning needs and achievement of each student. You and your co-teaching partner must shift perspective from covering the curriculum to teaching so that each student is learning. The purpose of our book is to coach you through the perspective change—to allow you to see the image emerge and experience the wonderful rewards of co-teaching.

We have written this book to provide administrators, general and special education teachers, service providers, interdisciplinary team members, and others who are co-teaching with practical, research-based, proven, and successful ways to approach this endeavor. District-level special or general education personnel who support site-based co-teaching may find the text as a helpful guide in their mentoring efforts. Even educators in nonteaming situations may benefit from the instructional ideas presented here. The text draws on the experience of co-teachers in the field who are seeing positive results from working side by side with their colleagues. You will also see how co-teachers blend their interpersonal skills and instructional expertise to support all children in the general education classroom. You will read case studies from teachers at various levels and in various subjects who have struggled with working with their partners and in finding ways to make co-teaching work. In other words, you will benefit from the lessons learned from the field. In short, we share the realities of co-teaching.

This book is different from other books on co-teaching as we blend the art of co-teaching with the research-based science of effective instructional methods. We include a model of co-teaching that emphasizes interpersonal skills, content knowledge, instructional design, teaching philosophy, and the stages of co-teaching. Each of these components must be considered when co-teaching.

Chapters include activities, checklists, and lesson plans, which you may find helpful as you plan and assess your co-teaching endeavors. Up-to-date chapter resources are included to guide your efforts, as well.

Chapter 1 provides an overview of co-teaching, which provides a framework for the remaining chapters. In Chapter 1, you will learn the definition of co-teaching, the components and prerequisites of co-teaching, and our model of co-teaching. Chapter 2 presents common issues and concerns and possible solutions to those issues. The remaining chapters provide examples of co-teachers at various grade levels teaching various subjects with varying levels of expertise with co-teaching who are using effective, research-based instructional methods. Each chapter emphasizes research-based instructional methods and effective interpersonal skills as the co-teaching team seeks to address an issue. We trust that the examples will inform your co-teaching practice.

Acknowledgments

Corwin Press would like to acknowledge the following people for their contribution to the book:

Rachel Aherns
Special Education Teacher
West Des Moines Community Schools
West Des Moines, IA

James Becker
English-Language Learners Teacher
St. Paul Public Schools
St. Paul, MN

Megan Reece
First-Grade Teacher
Rocky River Elementary School
Monroe, NC

Beverly E. Schoonmaker Alfeld, MA, MFA
Educational Consultant
Crystal Lake, IL

About the Authors

 **Greg Conderman, EdD,** is associate professor of special education at Northern Illinois University in DeKalb, Illinois, where he teaches methods and collaboration courses for elementary education, secondary education, and special education majors. Dr. Conderman was a middle and high school special education teacher and special education consultant for 10 years before entering higher education. He has authored over 50 articles on instructional methods and collaboration, which have been published in special education and general education journals. He is a frequent presenter at local, state, and national conferences. He has also received teaching awards for excellence in instruction at the college level.

 **Val Bresnahan, EdD,** is an adjunct instructor of special education at Northern Illinois University, where she teaches graduate and undergraduate courses in learning disabilities and inclusion. Dr. Bresnahan has taught elementary, middle, and high school students in special and inclusionary environments, and she has been a learning facilitator and a speech-language pathologist. In addition to teaching college courses, she is a middle school co-teacher in language arts and social studies in a central Illinois suburb. She has authored books and articles on vocabulary instruction and co-teaching and is a frequently invited presenter on reading and language skills.

 **Theresa Pedersen, MAT,** is a general education middle school language arts co-teacher in Rockford, Illinois. She has years of experience as an elementary education teacher, middle school resource teacher, high school special education teacher, and college instructor. She has co-authored articles on inclusion and student teaching. She has received awards for her excellence in instruction at the college level and was the recipient of the student teacher of the year award during her internship semester.

1

Taking the Plunge

What Is Co-Teaching All About?

All across the nation, general and special education teachers, English as second language teachers, and other service providers, such as speech-language pathologists from all grade levels and all content areas, are taking the plunge into co-teaching. Many of these teachers have had little or no preparation in this approach, so they are learning about co-teaching largely through trial and error. Perhaps their administrator informed them that they would be co-teaching, and therefore, they did not have much say in the matter, or maybe they volunteered for this new way of providing instruction to students. In either case, with little guidance or advice, they—perhaps like you—have taken the plunge into co-teaching.

The good news is that taking this plunge does not need to be a scary, dreadful, or uninformed experience. Many resources, examples, and real cases from the field are now available that can inform our practice. In short, we can learn from the experiences of others who have taken the plunge before us.

This book is intended to illustrate effective co-teaching practices and provide a road map for those who have—or will—take the co-teaching plunge. After reading this introductory chapter, you will be able to do the following:

- Offer a definition of co-teaching.
- Describe what co-teaching is and is not.
- Explain prerequisites for co-teaching.
- Propose reasons for co-teaching.
- Describe co-teaching stages.
- Articulate a model of co-teaching.

We invite you to take the plunge into the exciting and rewarding experience of co-teaching.

■ WHAT IS CO-TEACHING?

One widely accepted definition of *co-teaching* from Friend & Cook (2007) is the following:

> Co-teaching occurs when two or more professionals jointly deliver substantive instruction to a diverse, blended group of students in a single physical space. (p. 113)

The four parts of this definition, as well as the examples we share in this book, provide the context for our discussion of co-teaching. First, co-teaching involves *two or more certified teachers.* Usually we think of co-teaching as involving a general and special educator, but given the definition above, co-teaching can occur between or among two or more special educators, two or more general educators, or two or more other certified professionals. Many certified service providers, such as speech-language pathologists, school social workers, physical or occupational therapists, and English as second language teachers, now provide their services or support in the general education classroom rather than pulling students out for services. This approach often provides greater opportunities for more integrated learning for students, rather than focusing on isolated skills in a totally different context. Integrated services allow for immediate application and natural assessment of critical skills. While in the general education classroom, these professionals may coplan and copresent lessons applicable to all the students in the class. For example, a speech language pathologist might join general educators in selecting and preteaching vocabulary words for an upcoming unit. Mastering the vocabulary words is critical for all the students in the classroom—not just those with special needs. As noted, co-teaching often involves a special educator and a general educator. In fact, many special educators co-teach with several different general educators every day.

Second, the definition of co-teaching notes that these professionals *jointly deliver substantive instruction* to students. In other words, both professionals are meaningfully involved in the delivery of instruction, and instruction reflects recommended practices in the field. This is critical with the emphasis on research-based instructional practices under No Child Left Behind (NCLB) and the Individuals with Disabilities Education Act (IDEA). With two or more professionals in the room, the instruction should be qualitatively different than if you were teaching the class by yourself. With others in the room, perhaps different instructional grouping systems, different technologies, and varied assignments can be used that would be difficult—or impossible—to implement with just one teacher. Many co-teachers report that they are able to use approaches they could not implement on their own, perhaps due to classroom management or other issues. Co-teaching allows teachers to explore new or different ways of teaching all students.

Third, co-teaching occurs in *diverse classrooms.* A major tenant of co-teaching is that two teachers can better meet the needs of students in diverse, inclusive classrooms. According to Turnbull, Turnbull, Shank, and Wehmeyer (2007) inclusion seeks to ensure a place for all students in the general education curriculum to the maximum extent appropriate for each child, and professional collaboration is the strategy that advances inclusion and enhances the likelihood of its success. Clearly, IDEA creates a presumption in favor of educating students with disabilities with those who do not have disabilities. A clear progressive trend toward greater inclusion has been witnessed since 1984–1985, when the U.S. Department of Education first started collecting inclusion data (U.S. Department of Education, 2001). The shared expertise of both teachers is needed to differentiate or individualize instruction in such classrooms. However, not every inclusion class will have a co-teacher. Many districts have guidelines regarding the number or percentage of students with disabilities placed into a general education class that warrants a co-teacher.

Finally, co-teaching occurs *within a shared physical space.* Although on occasion, one teacher may remove a student or small group from the main instructional area for a specific purpose, such as remediation or assessment, both teachers and all students typically share a common physical space for the majority of instruction. Consistently separating or removing the same students from their peers, even if their instruction is different, is inconsistent with the co-teaching model. Further, both teachers should have equal opportunities to plan and provide instruction to all students within the same space. Clearly, the special education teacher was not placed in the inclusion classroom only to teach the students with disabilities.

WHAT CO-TEACHING IS NOT ■

Based on the co-teaching definition, then, we propose that co-teaching is not any of the following:

- Teaching with a paraprofessional, volunteer, or other noncertified assistant
- Implementing the same lessons in the same way you taught when you did not have a co-teacher
- Having two certified teachers provide instruction to a homogeneous class
- Grouping students with disabilities or language differences to work with the special education teacher or the English as a second language teacher at the back table or removing them to receive instruction in their special or separate classroom

WHAT ARE SOME ■
PREREQUISITES FOR CO-TEACHING?

Many people view co-teaching as being like a marriage. Therefore, co-teaching, like any collaborative relationship, rests on the following principles.

Parity

A co-teaching partnership is based on a spirit of equality. Years of teaching experience, degree, or age do not place one teacher in a higher position of authority over the other. Decisions are made mutually and are mutually agreed upon. Each teacher has an equal role in planning, executing, and evaluating the lesson. Admittedly, teachers have different strengths, skills, experiences, and knowledge to bring to the co-teaching experience, and these should not be minimized. Co-teachers should capitalize on the strengths of each partner without having one monopolize or succumb to the other based on perceived inequality.

Mutual Respect

Co-teachers need to be respected for their unique skills. Often, general educators have skill and experience with whole group instruction, group management systems, inquiry- or problem-based learning, and specific content knowledge within the general education curriculum. Special educators often have skills and experience in individualizing instruction, developing individual behavior systems, diagnosing, and sequencing skills. When their knowledge and skills are respected within a spirit of parity, both teachers are free to offer their areas of expertise and creative ideas without fear or humiliation.

Specific Mutual Goals

Co-teaching rests on shared goals. First and foremost, these goals are student based. Student-based goals often refer to increased academic skills, improved behavior or social skills, or increased access to the general education curriculum. Admittedly, co-teachers may be operating from different standards. For example, a math teacher may be using math standards, while an English as a second language (ESL) teacher may be using ESL standards. Through collaboration, lessons would apply to both sets of standards. Specifically articulating student goals early in the co-teaching partnership provides direction and purpose for co-teaching and offers a measure of accountability and growth. Co-teachers may also have professional reasons for co-teaching, such as the enjoyment of learning from a peer and the camaraderie of working closely with a colleague. Certainly, one advantage of co-teaching is professional growth from sharing ideas, strategies, methods, and materials.

Shared Accountability for Outcomes

When co-teachers teach, they become joint owners of the classroom. No longer is this "Mr. Ginther's classroom" or "the IEP kids" or "Miss Kristie's students." Similarly, the lesson is not "Mr. Ginther's lesson," even if he took a lead in developing it. If the lesson was successful, both teachers celebrate. Likewise, if the lesson was unsuccessful, both teachers reflect on what could be done differently in the future. In co-teaching, both teachers share instructional and behavioral accountability for all students.

Shared Resources

Have you known a teacher who hoarded materials and ideas, primarily so she would look good? We have. Some teachers resist sharing their creative ideas with others, but because co-teaching rests on the ideals of parity and shared accountability, a co-teaching partnership is characterized by openly sharing materials, ideas, methods, strategies, and approaches. For example, the general educator should feel free to share an activity that has been successful with students in the past. Similarly, the special educator may be aware of ways to modify written work for students who have hand writing, fine motor, or written language issues. The shared resources and expertise of both teachers embody the spirit of co-teaching. Figure 1.1 shows a visual summarizing these co-teaching requisites.

Figure 1.1   Visual of Co-Teaching Requisites

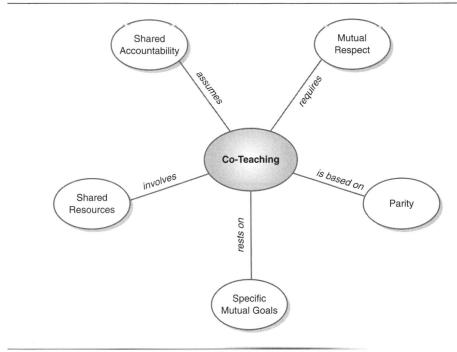

ADDITIONAL FACTORS TO CONSIDER   ■
BEFORE TAKING THE PLUNGE

Co-teaching does not occur in a vacuum, and successful co-teaching does not occur overnight. Some additional factors to consider when co-teaching include the following.

School Climate

Is your school characterized by a spirit of collaboration? Do teachers already freely share ideas and resources? Are students with disabilities considered part of the general population and, therefore, everyone's responsibility? If a collaborative culture does not already exist, co-teaching may be more challenging. Roy and O'Brien (1989) developed ten statements for individuals or teams to consider as they reflect on the collaborative nature of their school. The statements include the following:

1. The staff share a common language about instructional techniques.

2. The staff often observe each other in their classrooms and offer feedback about instruction.

3. The staff frequently discuss instructional techniques and methods.

4. The staff work together to master new instructional methods or strategies.

5. The staff plan and design educational materials together.

6. The staff pool expertise and share resources with each other.

7. The staff learn from and with each other.

8. Time is devoted during staff meetings to demonstrate and discuss innovative educational techniques, materials, and strategies.

9. Discussion in the staff lounge or workroom focuses mostly on instructional practices rather than social issues or student complaints.

10. Time is specifically provided for professional staff to plan and problem solve together.

We encourage grade-level and department teams, as well as the entire staff, to review these statements as they evaluate their school culture.

Administrative Support

Do your administrators support the co-teaching model? Will they provide necessary planning time and resources? Will they advocate for you if parents or other teachers have concerns about this model? Will they listen to issues regarding the co-teaching situation and offer support and guidance if you have unresolved conflict? Villa, Thousand, and Nevin (2004) note that administrators can ensure that all faculty receive appropriate training in collaborative planning, co-teaching models, differentiation, universal design, and cooperative learning; co-teachers are offered incentives receive needed resources; and state department personnel, faculty of institutions of higher education, and personnel from school districts form partnerships. Further, these authors note that administrators can support co-teaching by publicly articulating the rationale for co-teaching, redefining staff roles, assessing the staff's need for collaboration, creating a master schedule that allows for collaboration, and educating others about the accomplishments of collaborative planning and teaching teams. Administrators can also provide access for both teachers to student files, grading programs, and other student information that is critical for instructional purposes.

Parent Support

How do parents feel about the co-teaching model? Have you involved them? Have you supplied them with information about co-teaching on your Web site, through flyers or by other means? Do they understand how co-teaching is different from other, perhaps previously implemented special education instructional models? Involving parents in and informing and educating them about co-teaching empowers them to be equal partners in articulating the needs of their children.

Student Perspective

Have student needs—rather than the co-teaching model—dictated student Individualized Education Plans (IEPs)? Have you considered student needs and preferences when assigning students to the co-taught classroom? Have you prepared all students for the co-teaching approach?

Just as most adults appreciate being prepared for and involved with change, students also appreciate being involved in changes that affect them.

Personal Characteristics

Are you really ready or prepared to co-teach? Do you have the personal characteristics that enable you to work well with another adult in a shared space? Can you provide a safe learning environment—not only for students but also for your co-teacher? Are you willing to share "your" classroom and materials with someone else? What are you willing to give up to co-teach? Reflect on your co-teaching readiness by taking the survey in Figure 1.2, Willingness and Readiness for Co-Teaching.

WHY SHOULD I CO-TEACH? ■

Teachers co-teach for a variety of reasons. Following are some of them:

- Their administrator told them they had to (probably not the best reason).
- They believe that students with disabilities can learn more by remaining in the general education classroom with supports joining them.
- They believe students without disabilities also benefit from co-teaching.
- They have not been pleased with the results from their pull-out special education service delivery model.
- Their school district embraces inclusive practices.
- They believe they have skills that benefit all students.
- They are excited about working with all students.
- They want to grow professionally by learning from and with another colleague.

WHAT ARE THE CO-TEACHING STAGES? ■

Co-teaching is first and foremost a relationship. Like any relationship, co-teaching moves though stages, from the first "getting to know you" stage to the final "thinking as one" stage. The relationship develops as co-teachers get to know each other, build their trust and common repertoire, and work toward the final goal of collaboration. As in any relationship, teachers will experience different starting points and different timetables. Sometimes teachers volunteer to co-teach together. In this situation, the relationship probably started long before the co-teaching experience, even though that relationship may only have been social. At the other extreme, co-teachers with only a nodding acquaintance, if any, may be assigned to teach together. In this situation, the teachers must build their relationship from scratch.

Knowing the co-teaching stages is helpful, so you can identify where you are, the challenges you will face, and actions you can take to meet them to advance to the next stage. Some co-teaching partnerships move through the phases quickly, arriving at the final "thinking-as-one" stage in a few months, while others take several years of working together to get to this stage. Much depends upon where the relationship was when co-teaching began.

Gately and Gately (2001) identify three stages of co-teaching: beginning, compromising, and collaborating. Co-teachers with a limited work relationship prior to the co-teaching experience will start at the beginning

Figure 1.2   Willingness and Readiness for Co-Teaching

Rate yourself on the following scale: 1 = very   2 = somewhat   3 = not

How willing am I to . . .	*1*	*2*	*3*
• Work closely with another teacher?			
• Spend time coplanning and discussing activities and lessons?			
• Have someone else in the classroom while I am teaching?			
• Have someone else watch me teach?			
• Have someone else teach content to students?			
• Compromise on how things should be done in the classroom in terms of instruction?			
• Compromise on how things should be done in the classroom in terms of management?			
• Compromise on how things should be done in the classroom in terms of assessment of student learning?			
• Compromise on how things should be done in the classroom in terms of overall structure and expectations?			
• Compromise about classroom procedures?			
• Collaborate with someone else to make good decisions concerning curriculum?			
• Collaborate with someone else to make good decisions concerning management?			
• Collaborate with someone else to make good decisions concerning assessment of student learning?			
• Include a special education perspective on teaching and management?			
How prepared am I to work with children with disabilities?			
How comfortable am I having a special education teacher in the classroom observing and modifying current curricular instruction and behavioral practices?			

Source: Stump, C. S. (1999, March). *Understanding collaboration: What makes it work?* Paper presented at the Spring Tonic Conference at Silver Lake College, Manitowoc, WI.

stage and probably progress through the stages more slowly than teachers with a previously established relationship. This is to be expected. Care must be taken to understand the developmental progression of co-teaching and accept the realities and challenges of each stage.

Beginning Stage

This stage is the "getting-to-know-you" stage, in which you attempt to establish a new relationship—that of co-teachers. As in any relationship, this stage brings a certain amount of awkwardness as you get to know yourself and your co-teaching partner from a new perspective. If you are the general education teacher, you may feel rather possessive toward your classroom, students, and subject matter. This is normal and to be expected. After all, this has been your classroom for a number of years, and you are the content area expert. You may sense that the "other teacher" is intruding. Conversely, if you are the special education teacher, you may feel like an unwelcome guest: unimportant, excluded, and not in control of the situation. You may feel that you are at the whim of the general education teacher, following his lead, without opportunity for meaningful professional input. Often, at this stage, special education teachers report they feel more like instructional assistants than teachers. Indeed, at this level, often parents and students consider the "other teacher" to be the helper rather than a teacher.

One obvious indication of this stage is the use of space. Typically, the "other teacher" is relegated to a certain spot in the classroom, usually in the back, with little sense of ownership of space or access to materials. As Gately and Gately (2001) so aptly note, "There often appear to be invisible walls separating the space of the two teachers" (p. 41).

Communication at this stage may be polite, avoiding areas of conflict, as you both attempt to establish your fledging relationship. As one colleague noted, you may feel paralyzed, unable to move forward, because you really do not know what to do. However, realize that this getting-to-know-you beginning stage is normal and critical to the overall success of the co-teaching partnership. If you can get through the "opening willies," freely acknowledge your difficulties, and have understanding and empathy for your partner, you will be able to progress to the next stages. If you cannot begin an open honest dialogue, however, you may remain at this level, which will be very unsatisfying for both of you. The keys to success at this level are honesty, empathy, communication, and—above all—patience.

Compromising Stage

This stage is characterized by a "my-turn-your-turn" relationship. A "you teach this, and I will teach this" teaching arrangement may be seen at this level. Co-teachers may decide to divide teaching responsibilities, each taking charge of a certain curricular area. Professional communication is more expanded than in the beginning stage but not as fully established and interdependent as in the collaborative stage. The use of space changes slightly, as the "other teacher" moves to a different area of the classroom to teach a segment of the lesson, but that teacher often returns to her relegated spot. The "other teacher" rarely takes center stage, but territoriality becomes less evident (Gately & Gately, 2001). At this stage, students recognize both partners as teachers, but they still clearly identify one as the main teacher and the other as the "helper teacher."

Collaborative Stage

This is the jewel of co-teaching. At this level, both teachers are truly collaborative, often thinking as one. Here, the "image emerges," and the wonderful rewards of co-teaching begin. Both partners experience a high comfort level, humor, communication, and acceptance. Students, parents, and classroom visitors often are unable to distinguish the special education from the general education teacher. Both teachers are fluid, move around the classroom, occupy all spaces, and interact with all students. You can identify your co-teaching stage by viewing the Stages of Co-Teaching chart, shown in Figure 1.3.

You may find that your relationship has several characteristics in more than one section. That means you are moving forward. If all your characteristics are in one section, you may be "stuck." You need to identify an area to work on and get moving! Co-teachers may also want to track their progress by using the "How Are We Doing?" form, given in Figure 1.4. Independently, each co-teacher completes the form and shares his perceptions with his partner. Completed forms can be used as talking points for developing future co-teaching goals. Also, the variables on this form can be modified to reflect areas important to you and your co-teacher.

■ OUR MODEL OF CO-TEACHING

Many variables contribute to the success or failure of the co-teaching experience. Sometimes two teachers just do not get along—that is, their personalities are so different that co-teaching is a struggle rather than a joy. Perhaps one teacher is very controlling or another is gossipy. Perhaps the two teachers' communication styles are vastly different. In these instances, interpersonal issues may interfere with the co-teaching endeavor. Therefore, one component of our model of co-teaching involves each teacher's interpersonal skills. In this component of our model, we include the teacher's communication skills, approach to conflict, social skills, listening skills, and use of humor or sarcasm. You can imagine the difficulty a quiet, timid, serious teacher would have while co-teaching with a colleague who is bold, loud, and "in your face." We tend to like and work well with people who are like us—and we tend to be less comfortable with those who behave in ways that are vastly different than our own. Clearly, co-teachers need to be aware of their own interpersonal styles and the styles of their partners. They also need to be willing to modify their interpersonal styles, as needed, to make co-teaching work and make their partners welcome and comfortable. In short, co-teachers need to be aware of their own communication styles and those of their partners'. Figure 1.5 provides a communication skills survey for both co-teachers to complete before co-teaching to assess their communication styles. Knowing your own communication style and your strengths, needs, and weaker areas—as well as those of your partner—is a necessary initial step in taking the co-teaching plunge, so that misunderstandings can be minimized.

Another component in successful co-teaching is each teacher's content knowledge—or area of expertise. General education teachers—especially those at the middle or high school level—have expertise in one or more content areas, such as math or science. They enjoy the study of their discipline and are very knowledgeable in their content areas. In contrast, special educators or other service providers typically do not have expertise in a particular content area. Their preparation focused on methods that

Figure 1.3   Stages of Co-Teaching

	Beginning	Compromising	Collaborative
Description	Getting-to-know-you	My-turn, your-turn	Thinking-as-one
Interpersonal relationship	Awkward, guarded, and polite; limited professional discussions	Increase in professional communication; some give-and-take	Humor, comfort, ongoing; interdependent
Physical space	Limited mobility, back of the room	Some mobility but not center stage; return to relegated spot	Space jointly owned
Familiarity with curriculum	Special ed teacher unfamiliar with content or methodology; general teacher reluctant to release control, has lack of confidence in special ed teacher's skills	Special ed teacher beginning to have some knowledge of some curricular areas; general teacher becoming more confident of special ed teacher's skills	Both teachers fully appreciate the competencies each brings to co-teaching.
Materials	Special ed teacher has no access; brings own materials	Limited access to some materials	Full access to everything in the room
Recognized as . . .	Helper	Assistant teacher	Both are recognized as main teachers. Students accept both teachers as equal partners.
Students with whom you work	Special ed teacher only works with and only responsible for students with disabilities. "My kids, your kids" mentality prevails.	Special ed teacher may work with some students without disabilities, but he is still primarily responsible for students with IEPs. Special ed teacher may be seen as able to work with students who need support, but students who are higher performers remain the concern of the general ed teacher.	Both teachers work with all students. Both teachers responsible for the success of all students. "Our class, our students" mentality.
Planning	Limited to no joint planning, special ed teacher has limited to no knowledge of how lesson is organized or the lesson goals.	Some joint planning with general ed teacher taking the lead or each teacher taking responsibility for different sections of the lesson.	Teachers share responsibility for planning. Both are aware of the lesson goals and are responsible for making modifications for all students.
Service delivery	Separate curriculum taught to students with disabilities in the back of the room. Special ed teacher circulates and assists students with disabilities as needed.	Alternate teaching. Teachers divide the responsibility for planning and delivering specific lesson segments to the entire group. Special ed teacher may offer mini lessons or clarify strategies.	Both teachers participate in the presentation of the lesson and provide instruction to the entire group. Extra instruction or mini lessons are provided equally by both teachers.

Figure 1.4   Progress Check: How Are We Doing?

Date: _____   Co-Teachers: _____

Directions: Independently rate your perceptions of the co-teaching situation in the following areas using this scale: (1) I am feeling confident in this category, and no changes are needed at this time; (2) I am doing OK in this category, but we need to collaborate a bit more here; (3) I am feeling less confident in this category and need some assistance. In the final column, note conclusions from your discussion regarding your plan to address any concerns.

Category	My thoughts (1, 2, or 3)	My co-teacher's thoughts (1, 2, or 3)	Plan to address concerns:
Parity in the co-teaching relationship			
Communication between co-teachers			
Knowledge about the curriculum			
Instructional methods			
Classroom management			
Student achievement			
Other: List			
Other: List			

help students with disabilities overcome or compensate for their disability and that help such students access the general education curriculum. Therefore, co-teachers may find themselves with different levels of preparedness, familiarity, and comfort in core subjects. Clearly, though, each teacher has a strong skill set to bring to co-teaching.

Some co-teachers use effective and open communication skills and respect each other's difference in content preparation, but they are unsuccessful in

Figure 1.5   Communication Styles Inventory

This is an informal survey designed to determine how you usually act in everyday situations. The goal is to get a clear description of how you see yourself. On a sheet of paper, circle *A* or *B* in each pair of statements below, indicating the one that *most* describes you.

1. (A) I am usually open to getting to know people personally and establishing relationships with them.
   (B) I am not usually open to getting to know people personally and establishing relationships with them.

2. (A) I usually react slowly and deliberately.
   (B) I usually react quickly and spontaneously.

3. (A) I am usually guarded about other people's use of my time.
   (B) I am usually open to other people's use of my time.

4. (A) I usually introduce myself at social gatherings.
   (B) I usually wait for others to introduce themselves to me at social gatherings.

5. (A) I usually focus my conversations on the interests of people involved, even if that means straying from the business or subject at hand.
   (B) I usually focus my conversations on the tasks, issues, business, or subject at hand.

6. (A) I am usually not assertive, and I can be patient with a slow pace.
   (B) I am usually assertive, and at times I can be impatient with a slow pace.

7. (A) I usually make decisions based on facts or evidence.
   (B) I usually make decisions based on feelings, experiences, or relationships.

8. (A) I usually contribute frequently to group conversations.
   (B) I usually contribute infrequently to group conversations.

9. (A) I usually prefer to work with and through others, providing support when possible.
   (B) I usually prefer to work independently or dictate the conditions in terms of how others are involved.

10. (A) I usually ask questions or speak tentatively and indirectly.
    (B) I usually make empathic statements or directly expressed opinions.

11. (A) I usually focus primarily on ideas, concepts, or results.
    (B) I usually focus primarily on persons, interactions, and feelings.

12. (A) I usually use gestures, facial expression, and voice intonations to emphasize points.
    (B) I usually do not use gestures, facial expressions, and voice intonations to emphasize points.

13. (A) I usually accept others' points of view (ideas, feelings, and concerns).
    (B) I usually don't accept others' points of view (ideas, feelings, and concerns).

14. (A) I usually respond to risk and change in a cautious or predictable manner.
    (B) I usually respond to risk and change in dynamic or unpredictable manner.

15. (A) I usually prefer to keep personal feelings and thoughts private, sharing only when I wish to do to.
    (B) I usually find it natural and easy to share and discuss my feelings with others.

16. (A) I usually seek out new or different experiences and situations.
    (B) I usually choose known or similar situations and relationships.

17. (A) I am usually responsive to others' agendas, interests, and concerns.
    (B) I am usually directed toward my own agendas, interests, and concerns.

18. (A) I usually respond to conflict slowly and indirectly.
    (B) I usually respond to conflict quickly and directly.

(Continued)

Figure 1.5 (Continued)

Answer Sheet

O	G	D	I
1A	1B	2B	2A
3B	3A	4A	4B
5A	5B	6B	6A
7B	7A	8A	8B
9A	9B	10B	10A
11B	11A	12A	12B
13A	13B	14B	14A
15B	15A	16A	16B
17A	17B	18B	18A

TOTALS ＿＿＿ ＿＿＿ ＿＿＿ ＿＿＿

Total the numbers of items circled in each column and write that number on the spaces above.

Now, compare the *O* column with the *G* column and circle the letter that has the highest total:

O   or   G

Then compare the *D* column with the *I* column and circle the letter that has the highest total:

D   or   I

So What Is the Verdict?

If you circled the *G* and *D,* you tend toward being a Controller/Director.

If you circled the *O* and *D,* you show many qualities of a Promoter/Socializer.

If you circled the *O* and *I,* you are predominantly a Supporter/Relater.

If you circled the *G* and *I,* you have lots of Analyzer/Thinker characteristics.

Supporter/Relater

- Harmonizer
- Values acceptance and stability in circumstances
- Slow with big decisions; dislikes change
- Builds networks of friends to help do work
- Good listener; timid about voicing contrary opinions; concerned for others' feelings
- Easygoing; likes slow, steady pace
- Friendly and sensitive; no person is unlovable
- Relationship oriented

Analyzer/Thinker

- Assessor
- Values accuracy in details and being right
- Plans thoroughly before deciding to act
- Prefers to work alone
- Introverted; quick to think and slow to speak; closed about personal matters
- Highly organized; even plans spontaneity
- Cautious, logical, thrifty approach
- Thoughtful; no problem is too big to ponder
- Idea oriented

Promoter/Socializer

- Entertainer
- Values enjoyment and helping others with the same
- Full of ideas and impulsive in trying them
- Wants work to be fun for everyone
- Talkative and open about self; asks others' opinions; loves to brainstorm
- Flexible; easily bored with routine
- Intuitive, creative, spontaneous, flamboyant approach
- Optimist, nothing is beyond hope
- Celebration oriented

Controller/Director

- Commander
- Values getting the job done
- Decisive risk taker
- Good at delegating work to others
- Not shy but private about personal matters; comes on strong in conversation
- Likes to be where the action is
- Take-charge, enterprising, competitive, efficient
- Fearless; no obstacle is too big to tackle
- Results oriented

Source: Survey taken from Alessandra, T., & O'Connor, M. J. (1996). *The Platinum Rule.* New York: Warner Brooks. © Dr. Tony Alessandra 1976–2007. *"The Platinum Rule®"* is a registered trademark of Dr. Tony Alessandra. Used with permission. Adapted from Dr. Tony Alessandra's *Platinum Rule®* programs (www.alessandra .com/products/prrsproducts.asp). If you would like to take the *Platinum Rule* online assessment, visit www.platinumrule.com or call (330) 848-0444, ext 1.

co-teaching because of differences in teaching philosophy. This area includes each teacher's approach to learning and teaching; views on issues such as classroom management, grading, and assessment; and beliefs about the roles of the teacher and student. Imagine two teachers who communicate well but whose views on teaching and learning are vastly different. Perhaps one teacher believes strongly in inquiry-based instruction, while the other uses only a teacher-directed approach. Similarly, some teachers believe in grading every assignment, while others do not believe in grading at all. Some teachers expect all students to be able to monitor themselves regarding behavior and homework, while other teachers believe that such skills must be taught and modeled. Co-teachers need to communicate about these issues and reach agreement on what they can "live with" if they are going to share instructional responsibility for students.

A related component to address in co-teaching is one's specific teaching behaviors. Some teachers are very sequential and detailed in their instruction, while others focus on the big picture. Some teachers have a very relaxed approach, while others are more formal in their presentation. If the styles or approaches of two co-teachers differ greatly, students may have a difficult time negotiating the class. Although each teacher needs to be true to her own style and philosophy, effective teachers employ certain behaviors that have a greater likelihood of ensuring student success—especially in diverse classrooms.

As shown in Figure 1.6, the last component of our co-teaching model refers to the co-teaching stages. This is important to consider, because each stage has unique characteristics. Co-teachers in the beginning stage, for example, face different issues and challenges than those in more advanced stages. The stages indicate a developmental progression that co-teachers and administrators should consider when reflecting upon and assessing the co-teaching experience.

All of these components have one focal point—the academic achievement of each student. These co-teaching components—the interpersonal

Figure 1.6   Model of Co-Teaching

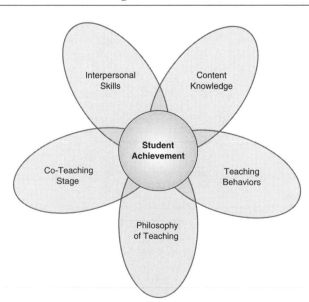

skills of co-teachers, content knowledge, teaching philosophy, teaching behaviors, and co-teaching stages—all share one measure of effectiveness: the achievement of *each, individual student* in the classroom. Co-teachers need to stay clearly focused on this vision. Teachers may need to revisit, retool, and refine each of the various components presented above, but the focus needs to be on students, their individual learning needs, and their achievements. Staying centered on students allows co-teachers to achieve the correct blend of the various components.

PUTTING IT ALL TOGETHER ■

Potential co-teachers can respond to questions developed by Murawski and Dieker (2004) for assessing the current environment, moving slowly, involving an administrator, knowing their partners, and creating a workable schedule as they begin initial planning toward their co-teaching efforts. Some of the questions in these categories include these:

1. What type of collaboration currently exists between general and special education?

2. What is our joint understanding of co-teaching as a service delivery model?

3. How will we ensure that support is provided across all content areas, including electives?

4. How shall we ensure that we both are actively involved and neither feels over or underutilized?

5. What schedule would best meet the needs of the class and both instructors?

SUMMARY ■

Co-teaching is an increasingly popular service delivery option that provides support to students in diverse inclusive classrooms. Co-teaching occurs when two or more professionals jointly deliver substantive instruction to a diverse, blended group of students in a single physical space. Because co-teaching is new, many teachers are taking the plunge and entering this professional partnership by trial and error.

The success of co-teaching rests upon both partners blending their instructional expertise and interpersonal skills. In addition, co-teaching requires that partners display parity and mutual respect, agree on specific mutual goals, and share accountability for outcomes and resources. These components are more likely to occur within a school climate that emphasizes collaborative relationships. Further, as in any relationship, co-teachers grow and become more comfortable with each other, the students, and their responsibilities over time. Co-teachers often follow a three-tiered developmental sequence. Teachers in the beginning stage are hesitant to make independent decisions due to their unfamiliarity with each other, and their interpersonal relationship may appear somewhat awkward. These teachers are still testing the waters. Teachers in the compromising stage are more comfortable with each other and their instructional responsibilities, and often they use the "my turn, your turn" approach. Finally, teachers in the collaborative stage experience a high level of comfort with each other and the curriculum, and their instruction is blended and fluid. Considering your co-teaching stage is important when reflecting upon and evaluating your co-teaching experience.

A model for co-teaching reflects these critical components by including each teacher's interpersonal skills, content knowledge, philosophy of teaching, teaching behaviors, and stage in the co-teaching experience. Co-teachers integrate these components as they stay clearly centered on the learning achievement of *each* student, which is the barometer of success of the co-teaching endeavor.

■ REFLECTIONS TO APPLICATION

As co-teachers, have we . . .

- Clarified what co-teaching is and is not?
- Examined prerequisites for co-teaching in our situation?
- Considered reasons why we are co-teaching?
- Assessed our current co-teaching stage?
- Discussed the co-teaching model presented here?

■ ADDITIONAL RESOURCES

Books

deBettencourt, L., & Howard, L. (2007). *The effective special education teacher: A practical guide for success.* Upper Saddle River, NJ: Pearson/Merrill-Prentice Hall.

Friend, M., & Cook, L. (2007). *Interactions: Collaboration skills for school professionals* (5th ed.). Boston: Pearson Education.

Villa, R. A., Thousand, J. S., & Nevin, A. I. (2004). *A guide to co-teaching.* Thousand Oaks, CA: Corwin Press.

Articles

Cook, L., & Friend, M. (1995). Co-teaching: Guidelines for effective practices. *Focus on Exceptional Children, 28*(3), 1–16.

Cramer, S., & Stivers, J. (2007). Don't give up: Practical strategies for challenging collaborations. *Teaching Exceptional Children, 39*(6), 6–11.

Friend, M., & Cook, L. (1992). The new mainstreaming. *Instructor 101*(7), 30–32, 34, 36.

Reinhiller, N. (1996). Co-teaching: New variations on a not-so-new practice. *Teaching Education and Special Education, 19*(1), 34–48.

Rice, N., Drame, E., Owens, L., & Frattura, E. (2007). Co-instructing at the secondary level: Strategies for success. *Teaching Exceptional Children, 39*(6), 12–18.

Wood, M. (1998). Whose job is it anyway? Educational roles in inclusion. *Exceptional Children, 64,* 181–195.

Videos

Burrello, L. C., Burrello, J. M., & Friend, M. (Producers). (2005). *The power of 2: Making a difference through co-teaching* (2nd ed.). [Video/DVD]. (Available from the Forum on Education, Indiana University, Smith Research Center, Suite 182, 2805 E. Tenth St., Bloomington, IN 47408).

2

Common Issues and Practical Solutions to Co-Teaching

Often the success or failure of co-teaching rests with the way logistics are handled—or not handled. Frequently, co-teachers have not thoughtfully considered the issues noted in this chapter, so they enter the co-teaching experience unprepared and with unrealistic expectations. Therefore, we offer this chapter on common issues and practical solutions associated with co-teaching. The issues and responses come from co teachers in the field and the co-teaching literature. For each issue, we offer various options for you to consider as you reflect on your co-teaching experience. After reading this chapter, you will be able to do the following:

- Describe various methods for getting started in co-teaching.
- List variables to be discussed by co-teachers before entering the co-teaching partnership.
- Brainstorm solutions to common issues faced by co-teachers.
- Illustrate common co-teaching models.
- Describe effective communication skills.
- Describe research-based instructional teaching behaviors.
- Identify ways to evaluate the co-teaching partnership.

MOVING FORWARD WITHOUT A MAP ■

Although recent graduates of teacher preparation programs may have learned about or even co-taught as part of their course work or field experiences, many seasoned teachers have not taken course work or field experiences that involved co-teaching. Fortunately, much has been written about co-teaching in the last decade. If you lack co-teaching preparation, or in other words you feel that you need to move forward but lack a road map, you could research co-teaching by completing Internet searches; checking resources in this text and other books; and viewing videos on co-teaching, such as the *Power of 2: Making a Difference Through Co-Teaching,* which was noted at the conclusion of Chapter 1. You could also contact your nearest college or university for courses, workshops, or seminars on co-teaching. You could also visit other co-teachers in your district or nearby districts: observing others co-teach may stimulate ideas for your own classroom, and asking them permission to call or e-mail with questions builds a support system as you begin your co-teaching venture.

■ BEGINNER CO-TEACHER CHALLENGES AND PRESSURES

Most teachers are prepared for—and expect to have—a classroom of their own. Sharing classroom space, materials, and ideas, as well as negotiating instructional methods and management styles, are challenges for beginner and experienced co-teachers. Typical pressures involve negotiating roles, ensuring student IEP goals and objectives are met, meeting the partner's expectations, and maintaining parity in the co-teaching partnership.

First and foremost, an important tip for addressing these challenges and pressures is to be authentic. In a professional manner, indicate what you need and want from the co-teaching situation. Pick your battles carefully—but approach your partner when something bothers you. Also, let your partner know your strengths and weaker areas, so you are not caught off guard. For example, perhaps you do not like last-minute changes or being called by your first name in front of students. Assume that your co-teacher is not purposefully doing these in a willful act of disrespect, but those actions probably will not change unless you address them. Openly discuss big issues (e.g., classroom management, planning, communication, grading curricular goals), as well as "nitty-gritty" details (e.g., specific responsibilities, how to handle specific student issues, who responds to parent concerns) before you begin co-teaching. Figure 2.1, Co-Teaching Issues for Discussion and Planning, and Figure 2.2, Sharing Hopes, Attitudes, Responsibilities, and Expectations, provide numerous questions and issues for co-teaching teams to discuss *before* they begin.

Co-teachers need to discuss the IEP goals of students with disabilities, as well as their accommodations or modifications and the reason for each. They should note language acquisition goals for students with language needs. To share accountability, maintain records and assessment data in convenient and accessible student files and frequently monitor student progress through informal assessments. During IEP meetings and annual reviews, examine the placement decision and effectiveness of the co-teaching model. One rating scale for assessing the co-teaching partnership is included as Figure 2.3. Each partner independently completes this form, and then both parties come together to share their perceptions. Partners can then develop a plan for addressing areas of concern.

We recommend that co-teachers reflect frequently upon the co-teaching experience. Possible questions to discuss include these: Are you both growing in understanding each other as well as the curriculum? Are you moving toward the collaborative stage in the co-teaching model? Are you using effective instructional techniques and appropriate communication skills?

Figure 2.1   Co-Teaching Issues for Discussion and Planning

Time for Planning

- How much time do we need?
- Where will we find the time we need?
- How will we use our time together?
- What records can we keep to facilitate our planning?

Instruction

- What content will we include?
- Who plans what content?
- How will we share teaching responsibility?
- Who adapts the curriculum and instructional and assessment procedures for select students?
- What are our strengths in the area of instruction and assessment?
- How will the content be presented: Will one person teach and the other(s) arrange and facilitate follow-up activities, or will all members share in the teaching of the lesson?
- How will we arrange to share our expertise? How can we arrange to observe one another and practice peer coaching?
- Do we rotate responsibilities?
- How will we assess the effectiveness of our instruction?

Student Behavior

- If we could each have only three class rules, what would they be?
- Who determines the disciplinary procedures?
- Who carries out the disciplinary procedures and delivers the consequences?
- How will we be consistent in dealing with behavior?
- How will we proactively address behavior?

Communication

- What types and frequency of communication do we like to have with parents?
- How will we explain this collaborative teaching arrangement to parents?
- Who will communicate with parents? Will there be shared responsibility for communication with parents of students who have identified special education or other specialized needs, or will particular members of the co-teaching team have this responsibility?
- Which types of communication do we like to have with students? With what frequency do we like to communicate with students?
- Who will communicate with students?
- How do we ensure regular communication with each other?
- Who communicates with administrators?

Evaluation

- How do we monitor student progress?
- How will we assess and grade student performance?
- Who evaluates which group of students: Do team members collaborate in evaluating all students' performances, or is each team member primarily responsible for evaluating a subset of students?

Logistics

- How will we explain our co-teaching arrangement to the students and convey that we are equals in the classroom?
- How will we refer to each other in front of the students?
- How will teacher space be shared?
- How will the room be arranged?
- Who completes paperwork for students identified as eligible for special education?
- How is the decision made to expand or contract team membership?
- How will a balance of decision-making power be maintained among co-teachers?

Figure 2.2   Sharing Hopes, Attitudes, Responsibilities, and Expectations

Directions: Both members of the co-teaching team address these questions independently. Be honest in your responses. After working independently, share your responses with your co-teacher. Jot down notes regarding what your partner says. After each has shared, develop an action plan and begin envisioning your future co-teaching classroom together.

		Action Plan
1.	**Right now, I regard this co-teaching situation as . . .**	
	My response:	
	Co-teacher response:	
2.	**My attitude/philosophy regarding students with disabilities in a general education classroom is . . .**	
	My response:	
	Co-teacher response:	
3.	**I would like to have these responsibilities in a co-taught classroom:**	
	I would like my co-teacher to have the following responsibilities:	
4.	**The biggest obstacle I expect to have in this partnership is . . .**	
	My response:	
	Co-teacher response:	
5.	**I have the following expectations in a classroom regarding . . .**	
	(a) discipline:	
	My response:	
	Co-teacher response:	
	(b) in-class activities:	
	My response:	
	Co-teacher response:	
	(c) homework:	
	My response:	
	Co-teacher response:	
	(d) planning:	
	My response:	
	Co-teacher response:	
	(e) modifications for individual students:	
	My response:	
	Co-teacher response:	
	(f) grading:	
	My response:	
	Co-teacher response:	
	(g) noise level:	
	My response:	
	Co-teacher response:	
	(h) cooperative learning:	
	My response:	
	Co-teacher response:	
	(i) providing student feedback:	
	My response:	
	Co-teacher response:	
	(j) receiving feedback from peers:	
	My response:	
	Co-teacher response:	
	(k) parent contact:	
	My response:	
	Co-teacher response:	

Source: Adapted from Murawski, W. W. (2003). Grades 6–12. In *Co-teaching in the inclusive classroom: Working together to help all your students find success* (pp. 36–37). Medina, WA: Institute for Educational Development.

Figure 2.3   Self Assessment: "Are We Really Co-Teachers?"

Directions: Respond to each question below to determine your co-teaching score at this point in time.

1. Rarely   2. Sometimes   3. Usually

In our co-teaching partnership . . .

1.	We decide which co-teaching model we are going to use based on the benefits to students and co-teachers.	1	2	3
2.	We share ideas, information, and materials.	1	2	3
3.	We identify the resources and talents of the co-teachers.	1	2	3
4.	We teach different groups of students at the same time.	1	2	3
5.	We are aware of what our co-teacher(s) is doing even when we are not directly in his or her presence.	1	2	3
6.	We share responsibility for deciding what to teach.	1	2	3
7.	We agree on the curriculum standards that will be addressed in a lesson.	1	2	3
8.	We share responsibility for deciding how to teach.	1	2	3
9.	We share responsibility for deciding who teaches parts of the lesson.	1	2	3
10.	We are flexible and make changes, as needed, during a lesson.	1	2	3
11.	We identify student strengths and needs.	1	2	3
12.	We share responsibility for differentiating instruction.	1	2	3
13.	We include others when their expertise or experience is needed.	1	2	3
14.	We share responsibility for how student learning is assessed.	1	2	3
15.	We can show that students are learning when we co-teach.	1	2	3
16.	We agree on discipline procedures and implement them together.	1	2	3
17.	We provide feedback to each other on what goes on in the classroom.	1	2	3
18.	We improve our lessons based on what happens in the classroom.	1	2	3
19.	We freely communicate our concerns.	1	2	3
20.	We have a process for resolving disagreements which we use when faced with challenges and conflicts.	1	2	3
21.	We celebrate the process, outcomes, and successes of co-teaching.	1	2	3
22.	We have fun with each other and the students when we co-teach.	1	2	3
23.	We have regularly scheduled times to meet and discuss our work.	1	2	3
24.	We use our meeting time productively.	1	2	3
25.	We effectively co-teach even without common planning time.	1	2	3
26.	We explain co-teaching benefits to students and their families.	1	2	3
27.	We model collaboration and teamwork for our students.	1	2	3
28.	We are both viewed by our students as their teacher.	1	2	3
29.	We include students in the co-teaching role.	1	2	3
30.	We depend on one another to follow through on responsibilities.	1	2	3
31.	We seek and enjoy additional training to improve our co-teaching.	1	2	3
32.	We are mentors to others who want to co-teach.	1	2	3
33.	We use various co-teaching models.	1	2	3
34.	We communicate our needs to our administrators.	1	2	3
35.	We respect and appreciate the contributions of our co-teacher.	1	2	3

Total co-teaching score: _____

■ WORKING WITH ADULTS

As a co-teacher, your primary responsibility is still teaching children—which is why you entered teaching. Co-teaching is all about delivering instruction to students. Co-teaching, however, does involve another layer, which is communicating and negotiating decisions with another adult. To maintain your focus and energy on students, consider enlisting the assistance of your co-teacher in revising assignments or activities that need updating. Avoid just using last year's lesson plans with this year's students and subjects. To invite collaboration, share instructional and assessment responsibilities with your partner. Maybe your partner will gladly assume some tasks you find unfulfilling, so you can focus your creative energy on tasks you enjoy. In other words, determine and capitalize on your partner's strengths in lesson plans and curriculum design. Incorporate various co-teaching models into short- and long-term lesson planning and ensure that both you and your partner have opportunities to teach all students. You can involve students by asking which co-teaching models they enjoy and what they like about having two teachers. Finally, co-teaching can be more rewarding when you remain current in your profession by joining your professional organization, reading journals, and attending workshops and conferences by yourself or with your teaching partner. Learning new methods to use in your classroom keeps your focus on students.

■ WANTING TO CO-TEACH

Perhaps your most comfortable style is to work independently. Actually, many teachers probably prefer to work independently. However, schools are becoming more collaborative—especially with the increase in diversity. If you feel reluctant or hesitant with the co-teaching approach, remember to begin slowly. Instead of committing yourself to having a co-teacher for one class period for the entire year, start by sharing your classroom with a colleague whom you trust. Perhaps this colleague can join you once a week for co-teaching. Hopefully, this positive experience with someone with whom you are comfortable will encourage you to increase your collaborative efforts. Reflect on your hesitation to co-teach with others. Be honest with yourself. Perhaps you are a beginning teacher and want the opportunity to teach your class by yourself, at least for a year or two before you begin co-teaching. Perhaps you are eying retirement, and you do not want to invest energy in new approaches right now. Maybe you do not get along with the special education teachers or service providers in your school, so co-teaching would add another layer of stress. Being honest is important: you can then decide if your hesitation is based on fear, resistance, or a more legitimate reason. Observe and "interview" others who have had positive experiences with co-teaching.

Perhaps you will not have to co-teach in your career. Not all general education or special education teachers co-teach. Some district administrators embrace co-teaching while others do not. Be sure to ask about this while you are interviewing or advancing in your district.

■ PLANNING ISSUES

Having time to plan together is a critical factor in effective co-teaching relationships. This is when co-teachers review the outcome of a lesson and plan subsequent instruction based on students' responses to the learning environment the co teachers have created. Without an opportunity for daily reflection and coplanning, co-teaching is often relegated to the one-lead, one follow format. Such a format often designates one teacher as the primary teacher and the other as "helper." Exclusive use of this co-teaching format can lead to burnout on the part of the "helper" teacher (Murawski, 2005). In addition, the instructional power of having two teachers with parity in the classroom is lost without co-planning.

To avoid this situation, before agreeing to co-teach, determine the amount of common planning time you have during the week. Most effective co-teaching teams find that weekly planning time of 40 to 45 minutes is insufficient, and they choose a common daily planning time (Scruggs, Mastropieri, & McDuffie, 2007). Having planning time in the schedule may be viewed as evidence of the level of administrative support. An administrator who understands and values the co-teaching model realizes the amount of additional planning this model necessitates and will advocate for teachers to get this time. Conversely, lack of time allocated for coplanning may indicate of lack of support. This alone may be a sufficient reason to abandon the co-teaching model.

Even with allocated planning time, co-teaching teams may need to meet beyond this scheduled time, especially during the first year. Consider these ten suggestions for finding critical additional planning time:

1. Meet before or after school or during lunch.

2. Use e-mail or designate a specific evening time for phone calls.

3. Meet once a week to coplan for the entire week.

4. Place your lesson plans on your Web site for you co-teacher to access.

5. Have a communication lesson plan folder or notebook that travels to and from each teacher's mailbox.

6. Use a common bulletin board to post lesson plans.

7. Every day, place a specific agenda on the board, so when your co-teacher enters, she can easily see the lesson plan.

8. When the co-teacher joins the class, restate the agenda and each teacher's responsibilities, promoting clarity for the co-teacher and students.

9. As part of the lesson conclusion—and before the co-teacher leaves for the day—state what will happen tomorrow as well as each teacher's role. This provides closure to the lesson, alerts students and the co-teacher regarding tomorrow's lesson, and helps orient the co-teacher for the following day.

10. Use time during class when students are working independently to communicate briefly with your co-teacher. Assign students a meaningful, independent activity, such as ten minutes of silent reading or responding to a journal prompt, and during that time, briefly review lesson objectives and procedures with your co-teacher. Friend and Cook (2007) offer a three-part coplanning process. The general education teacher does the first phase prior to the planning meeting by considering and outlining upcoming curricular content and instructional activities. In the second phase, both co-teachers review the material and decide how to arrange teachers and students to meet instructional goals. The special

educator takes the lead on the third phase by designing needed accommodations or modifications for students or groups.

■ DIFFERENT TEACHING STYLES, PERSONALITIES, AND PHILOSOPHIES

Ideally, co-teachers will be able to complement each other's teaching styles. Co-teaching does not require you to abandon your teaching style, favorite lesson, or philosophical approach to teaching and learning. Actually, co-teaching might be boring if both teachers viewed everything in exactly the same way. However, co-teaching does require that both teachers negotiate, compromise, and avoid making assumptions about their partners. Instead, specifically discuss your teaching philosophies, styles, and approaches to learning. Do you lean toward a constructivist approach or a teacher-directed approach? Are you open to other approaches—especially if your students learn best with a different approach? Will you allow your co-teacher to place his twist on the lesson as long as students learn the material? If, after you and your partner have thoroughly discussed your teaching approaches, you believe your views differ significantly, you may decide not to enter or continue co-teaching. Note when and where different styles or approaches may be appropriate for your students and use student data as a basis for making those decisions.

■ DEMONSTRATING PARITY

Parity is an essential ingredient of co-teaching. Both teachers need to feel respected and valued for their contributions. Co-teachers can maintain parity the following ways:

- Using phrases such as "our students" rather than "your students" or "the students who are included"
- Including both teachers' names on parent communications, Web pages, report cards, the classroom door, the school directory, and school publications, such as newsletters, class photos, and parent handbooks
- Sharing e-mails and other forms of communication
- Conferring with each other before sending a response to a parent, student, or administrator
- Equipping the classroom with a desk and space for each co-teacher
- Ensuring that both teachers teach all students and are responsible for the learning of all students by grading papers together, designing rubrics, and agreeing on report card grades before submission
- Referring to both teachers as teachers (not as a helper or assistant) and using the same title for both teachers, such as Mr. Ewing and Mrs. Gael, rather than Mr. Ewing and Wanda
- Supporting decisions of the co-teacher (especially in front of the students)

■ BEHAVIOR ISSUES

Teaching is a joy when expectations are clear to everyone and when students comply with those expectations. Similarly, consistently dealing with behavior issues is stressful and takes the joy out of teaching. As with other critical classroom components, co-teachers should specifically discuss classroom expectations, rules, and consequences for appropriate and inappropriate behavior. Post these rules or expectations as a visual reminder for everyone. Consider sending parents a handout summarizing classroom expectations and posting classroom rules on your Web site. Remind students that both teachers will be enforcing classroom rules in the same way.

Co-teachers can agree on a system ranking least to most severe consequences for inappropriate student behavior. For example, will you first give a verbal reminder or warning before administering a more severe consequence? Allow your co-teacher to reward and administer consequences and then support her decisions. If differences of opinions occur regarding discipline, privately discuss those differences with your co-teacher by referencing your previous discussions about classroom management. Remember that students with disabilities and lower achievers often require more encouragement and reinforcement, because the curriculum is more challenging for them. Sprick, Garrison, and Howard (1998) and others recommend that students with disabilities receive three positive comments per every reminder or negative comment. Monitor your interactions with students and set a goal to maintain this three-to-one ratio.

Remember to review student IEPs for any special behavioral accommodations, modifications, or intervention plans. Keep notes regarding those plans in a convenient place, such as your grade or lesson plan book. If you observe a student breaking a classroom rule and feel that you must react but are unsure what to do at that moment, consider enlisting the support of your co-teacher on the spot by saying something like, "Mrs. Sheldorf, I have given Les several reminders to raise his hand, and he continues to talk out. How do you suggest *we* handle this?" Another possibility is to let the student know a consequence will be given after both co-teachers have been consulted.

HANDLING CONFLICT ■

Conflict is inevitable in any close relationship. When conflict occurs, ask yourself how—or if—you want to address the issue. As in any relationship, think carefully about the consequences of both addressing and not addressing the conflict. First, we suggest that you decide when and if you should confront your partner. Is this a one-time type of problem, or has this been going on for some time? Consider the consequences of addressing the issue as well as ignoring the issue. Honestly reflect on why you are upset and why you want to confront your partner. What is your motive? Are you upset because the students are bonding better with your co-teacher? Are you jealous of the energy your co-teacher brings to the classroom? Do you feel you have no control over important issues that affect your position? Do not confront your partner with the issue when you are angry or upset. Take time to cool down. Sleep on it for at least one night.

If you decide to confront, remember that sensitive issues are best discussed in person rather than on the phone or through e-mail. Keep focused on the issue. Do not bring up past issues, personalities, or events. Use effective communication skills, such as those described below. Recall the main conflict styles: avoidance (do not confront), accommodation (give in to your partner's requests), compromise (meet halfway), force (it is my way or else), and collaboration (openly state your needs and see if a new solution can be reached). We have found that the compromise and collaboration approaches yield more success in co-teaching endeavors than other conflict approaches.

■ EFFECTIVE COMMUNICATION

Because effective co-teaching requires constant communication that enables partners to feel empowered and part of the process, co-teachers may wish to review effective communication skills. First, remember to use consistent signals when you communicate—verbal and nonverbal signals need to be in agreement. Also, be aware of limitations of certain forms of communication, such as e-mail, as the recipient cannot sense nonverbal signals, voice tone, and inflections. Some effective communication techniques include the following:

- Minimal encouragers such as "Hmmm, I see, yes, OK, uh-huh" signal to your co-teacher that you are listening and interested in what he has to say.
- Open-ended questions that begin with "How do you feel about . . . " "What are your thoughts on . . . " or "What do you think of . . . " are helpful in collaborative relationships as they elicit your partner's opinions, thoughts, or feelings.
- Response to affect statements are used to connect with your partner emotionally and empathize with her. These statements include a "feeling word," where the co-teacher anticipates how the partner feels about something by saying something like "You sound upset about . . ." or "I'd be frustrated, too, if . . ." or "Sounds like you are encouraged by . . . ."
- Paraphrasing is used when you want to check your understanding of the content (not emotion) of what your partner said. These statements are short summaries that often begin with "So, what you are saying is . . . " or you simply recap what your partner said.
- "*I* messages" are used to share how you feel about something specific that you have seen or heard. An *I* message contains three parts: (1) what you see or hear, (2) your feelings about what you saw or heard, and (3) the tangible effect those events have on you. *I* messages can be delivered to students or colleagues, they can have a positive or negative slant, and the three components can be placed in any order. Here are two examples:

  For students: "When I see you enter the classroom quietly, I am pleased because I can start our lesson immediately."

  For your co-teacher: "I feel disappointed when you do not maintain confidentialities, and now I have to call Mr. and Mrs. Svoboda and apologize to them."

- The sandwich technique is a three-part message that is often used to bring up a sensitive or negative issue with a parent or colleague. Place the issue in the middle of a message sandwich. The pieces of bread (the statements before and after the issue) soften the issue. Often the first statement presents a positive quality or positive statement or reaffirms a quality of caring. The last statement often requests assistance in addressing the issue or confirms the collaborative partnership. Here is an example: "Mrs. Romez, I know how much you care about your son. That is why I need to tell you I caught Roberto cheating on his spelling test today. I am wondering how we can work together to address this issue."

ADMINISTRATOR SUPPORT ■

An administrator's support is critical to co-teaching. Depending on their backgrounds, expertise, strengths, and skills, administrators can support co-teaching in the following ways:

- Suggesting teachers who they believe would be successful co-teaching partners
- Offering resources for co-teachers, such as books, articles, videos, or staff development opportunities
- Developing a school culture where collaboration is valued and expected
- Offering buildingwide training on collaboration and co-teaching
- Listening to and brainstorming with co-teachers regarding unique concerns or issues
- Advocating for co-teachers when and if others claim co-teachers have less work to do
- Explaining the co-teaching model to parents, students, and other teachers, as needed
- Assuring that co-teachers' teaching evaluations include and reflect their co-teaching experiences
- Establishing excellent models of co-teaching in their buildings that serve as examples for others
- Listening to both teachers and gathering information before taking action when conflict occurs
- Ensuring that co-teachers have a daily common planning time
- Having a vision for co-teaching based on the potential for helping students and teachers, rather than using co-teaching as a way to mentor a poorly performing teacher, justify large class sizes, or remain politically correct.

CO-TEACHING CAVEATS ■

Admittedly, co-teaching is not for every teacher or every student. Successful co-teaching relationships are built upon mutual trust and respect for each other's expertise. Compatibility with your co-teacher is essential. Even teachers who have volunteered to work together may realize they do not share compatible views in essential instructional areas. If you and your co-teaching colleague do not share a similar perspective on effective teaching, co-teaching may not be for you. Similarly, if you and your potential co-teaching partner have conflicting beliefs about how to manage behavior, plan for co-teaching, and interact with students, co-teaching, at least with each other, might not be effective or professionally rewarding.

Co-teaching may also not be the most appropriate teaching arrangement for all students. Students with attention concerns or considerable off-task behaviors may have difficulty attending in co-taught classrooms. Some students may not be able to bond with or divide their attention between two teachers. Students who do not have a minimum academic or behavioral skill level may not be able to meet the demands of a general education setting (Scruggs et al., 2007). These students may require extensive teacher assistance, which minimizes equal contributions to the co-teaching effort.

In an era when more districts are using co-teaching to meet the diverse needs of students, remember that co-teaching may not be the most effective model for everyone in every situation. Careful attention to the needs of both students and their teachers must be considered, so that co-teaching does not become the new "one-size-fits-all" solution.

■ CO-TEACHING MODELS

Researchers, such as Friend and Cook (2007), have shared several co-teaching models in the literature. Partners may wish to consider these as they plan instruction. These co-teaching models include the following:

- *One teach, one observe:* In this model, one teacher takes the lead role in presenting instruction to the whole class, while the partner assumes the more passive yet important role of collecting observational data on student behavior and participation or teacher behavior, such as who is being called on. This data can provide invaluable information that would be difficult to collect objectively without a co-teacher.
- *One teach, one drift:* In this model, one teacher takes the lead instructing the whole class, while the other assumes a more passive, supportive role by drifting, or circulating, around the classroom to support students or small groups. The support teacher might answer student questions, prompt students to get back on task, provide physical proximity as a proactive effort to reduce management issues, or help students get organized for the lesson.

These first two models tend to be used when common planning does not exist.

- *Parallel teaching:* In parallel teaching, the class is equally divided in two, and each teacher teaches the lesson to half the students. Both teachers use the same lesson plan to ensure that students in both groups are exposed to the same information.
- *Station teaching:* Several variations of station teaching exist. Usually, this model involves having several learning stations around the room with groups of students moving from station to station at strategic points. Often, one co-teacher coordinates one station, the other co-teacher coordinates another station, and the remaining station or stations include independent learning activities.
- *Alternate teaching:* If you have a small group of students who need review, reteaching, or acceleration, you could use alternate teaching. In this model, one teacher takes the lead in instructing the large group, while the other works with a smaller group off to the side for a special purpose. Be sure to vary the reasons for and composition of the small group, and each teacher should take turns as the lead and alternate co-teacher.
- *Team teaching:* Often cited as the ultimate goal of co-teaching, this model involves both teachers taking a lead in active instructional responsibilities. In team teaching, both teachers together may co-present a lesson. Both teachers are viewed as equal partners in instructional planning and delivery.

In addition to these models, co-teachers can support each other during transition times and other classroom events. Figure 2.4 provides some examples of purposeful activities that can be conducted by co-teachers during various instructional and noninstructional events.

Figure 2.4   Teacher Activities During the Co-Teaching Process

If YOU are doing this:	Your CO-TEACHER can be doing this:	Benefits of inclusion:
Presenting new information through lecture or media (PowerPoint, video or audio clip)	Modeling note taking on the board or overhead or filling in a graphic organizer	Content is accessible for all students. Strong connections are made between new and previously learned content. Student understanding is facilitated.
Taking attendance	Collecting or reviewing homework or introducing or reviewing a social or study skill	Instructional time is increased. Skill-based instruction is integrated into lessons. Student behaviors may improve.
Distributing papers	Reviewing directions or modeling the first problem on the assignment	Instructional time is increased. Examples promote student understanding and errorless learning.
Giving instructions orally	Writing down instructions on board or overhead or repeating or clarifying any difficult concept	Content is accessible for all students.
Checking for understanding with large, heterogeneous groups of students	Checking for understanding with small, heterogeneous groups of students	Reteaching can occur without delay.
Circulating, providing one-on-one support as needed	Providing direct instruction to the whole class	Learning is not left to chance. Student learning of errors is reduced.
Prepping half the class for one side of a debate	Prepping the other half of the class for the opposing side of the debate	Instructional time is increased. Student engagement is increased
Facilitating independent, silent work	Circulating and checking for comprehension	Reteaching can occur without delay.
Providing large-group instruction	Circulating, using proximity control for behavior management	On-task behavior is increased. Behavior referrals are decreased.
Reteaching or preteaching with a small group	Monitoring the large group as students work on practice materials	Student learning of errors is minimized.
Facilitating sustained silent reading	Reading aloud quietly with a small group or previewing upcoming information	Students internalize language and structures to apply to independent reading.
Reading a test aloud to a group of students	Proctoring a test silently with a group of students	IEP accommodation requirements are met without delay.
Creating basic lesson plans for standards, objectives, and content curriculum	Providing suggestions for modifications, accommodations, and activities for diverse learners	Student needs are met through differentiated instruction. Lessons are created to meet the needs of student subgroups.
Facilitating stations or groups	Facilitating other stations or groups	Instructional materials can be tailored to the needs of different students.
Explaining a new concept	Conducting role-play, modeling a concept, or asking clarifying questions	Student interest and motivation are increased. Students are engaged in critical thinking skills and develop inquiring attitudes.
Considering modification needs	Considering enrichment opportunities	Everyone works toward essential understandings and skills. More options are available to meet student needs.

Source: Adapted from Murawski, W. M., & Dieker, L. A. (2004). Tips and strategies for co-teaching at the secondary level. *Teaching Exceptional Children, 36*(5), 52–58.

■ EFFECTIVE TEACHING BEHAVIORS

Several research-based teaching behaviors or presentation techniques have been found to be effective for all students at all levels, but especially for learners considered at risk.

Teach for Understanding Rather Than Exposure

One principle is to *teach for understanding rather than exposure.* This powerful phrase—6 words and 12 syllables—is contrary to the way in which many teachers conduct lessons. This phrase holds the secret to successful teaching in both the traditional and co-teaching models. Often, teachers teach for exposure rather than in-depth understanding. To teach for understanding, teachers reduce textbook information to a few areas of critical understanding and design and present instruction around big ideas. Teachers can ask themselves questions such as "If my students only take one idea away from this unit, what would that be?" "What do I want them to remember ten years from now?" "What am I teaching that has universal application?" "What key concepts do I need to cover in depth?" and "How can I relate these key concepts to other lessons I have taught or to other disciplines?"

Determining big ideas helps you communicate your lesson's objectives with your co-teacher. In addition to providing a clear objective for co-teaching, determining big ideas is essential in planning lessons to accommodate the wide diversity within today's classrooms.

Explicit Instruction

Another effective teaching behavior is to use explicit instruction. After determining big ideas, share them with students and repeat them often. Start each lesson by telling students what they are going to learn, the rationale, and how new material is connected to what they have learned before. Always tell students exactly what you expect of them in terms they can understand. If you assign a final product, provide a good model or example before students begin working. Designing a rubric is a good way to be explicit about the range of your expectations. Apply the rubric to several models of student work within a range; keep the models in front of students, so they can compare their work against a standard; and refer to the models often while students complete the project.

Scaffolded Instruction

A third effective method is called scaffolded instruction. Here, you provide students with ongoing support as needed, but you gradually reduce the level of help you provide as students demonstrate competence in working independently. The three stages of scaffolding are as follows:

1. *Teacher modeling or "watch me do it."* At this beginning stage, the teacher shows and tells students what to do while demonstrating. Usually the teacher uses words such as "First, I will . . . ; next, I will . . . ; finally, I will . . ." Teacher think-alouds are effective in demonstrating expectations.

2. *Teacher and student together.* At this intermediate stage, the teacher provides assistance for students, gradually reducing teacher involvement

as students gain proficiency. In this stage, teachers may say, "Now, you do it with me," or "Let's do this together."

3. *Student alone.* At this final stage, the student performs the activity independently under the teacher's guidance.

These three steps are also referred to as "I do, we do, you do."

Errorless Learning

Teachers can also incorporate errorless learning into their presentations. Errorless learning means that instruction is presented at the level at which students can achieve success, with a minimal number of errors. Often teachers reframe, redesign, or rerepresent a learning task by teaching in smaller steps, providing more examples and nonexamples, using more visuals, and checking frequently for student understanding. Content area teachers may find the expertise of co-teachers particularly valuable when designing presentations that promote errorless learning.

Active Involvement of Students

Another effective teaching behavior is to actively involve students. Some techniques for involving students include promoting unison responding, using dry erase boards, and teaming students with a partner with whom to share a response before responding to the class. While one teacher presents the lesson, the co-teacher can circulate and monitor student written responses, allowing for immediate feedback. With this feedback, you can decide to reteach, provide more practice opportunities, or advance to the next skill or concept.

Providing Practice Opportunities

Effective teachers also provide numerous practice opportunities for students. Most of us forget how to complete tasks we seldom practice. This is especially true for many learners in diverse classrooms who need frequent opportunities to learn new skills and concepts. For maximum effectiveness, practice must be sufficient, varied, distributed, and integrated into new learning tasks. A benefit of co-teaching is the opportunity to discuss creative ways to provide students with repeated practice.

Monitoring of Teacher Presentation

Teachers can also monitor their teacher-talk and their pace. How often have you listened to someone but not understood a word he was saying? Perhaps he talked too fast, used words you never heard before, used very complicated sentence structure, or put so many ideas together that you simply could not follow what he was saying? Students in diverse classrooms may feel confused when teachers present too much verbal information in a short period. Often the content area specialist is so familiar with the concepts and has presented the lesson so many times that she uses vocabulary and sentence structure beyond students' comprehension level. Consider tape-recording yourself presenting a lesson. Take special note of your vocabulary. Are you sure all students understand your words? Similarly, teachers need to use proper pacing, which means that lessons are long enough to provide necessary scaffolding and repeated practice but quick enough to maintain student attention. Proper pacing also involves limited time spent on transitions, so that student contact time is maximized. In addition to recording themselves, teachers can monitor each other and then give feedback.

Giving Feedback to Students

Finally, effective teachers frequently assess and provide timely and corrective feedback to students. To know what to teach, you need to be aware of which students are learning and which students are falling behind. We realize this is a challenge, especially in single-teacher middle and high school classrooms, where teachers teach as many as 100 students each day. Providing timely corrective feedback to students can be more manageable in co-taught classrooms when teachers share assessment tasks, use various instructional models, and share student observations.

If you and your co-teaching partner continually review your teaching behaviors in light of these research-based principles, you will be well on your way to ensuring success for each student in your classroom.

■ SUMMARY

This chapter presented frequently noted issues about co-teaching and provided possible responses to those issues. Co-teachers frequently have questions about getting started on a positive note. A major theme in this chapter is the importance of initiating and maintaining respectful and honest communication between both partners.

Spending a considerable amount of time talking about pet peeves, teaching philosophies, classroom management, and what you want from the co-teaching experience—even before you begin—is a recommended proactive measure that will support your early discussions about important issues. However, having that important first discussion is just the starting point. Co-teachers need to maintain the dialogue as new issues, questions, and inevitable conflicts arise.

After dialoging about important issues, co-teachers may conclude that their differences cannot be resolved and that they should not advance toward co-teaching. In these situations, administrator support is critical.

This chapter also presented tips for addressing conflict and offered examples of effective communication skills, which represent the interpersonal component in our co-teaching model. Often, the success of co-teaching rests with both partners monitoring their verbal comments and nonverbal signals and checking to ensure that their message has been given and received in ways that value, honor, and promote the collaborative relationship. The chapter concluded by noting effective instructional behaviors that can be incorporated in classrooms regardless of grade level or subject matter.

REFLECTIONS TO APPLICATION ■

As co-teachers, have we . . .

- Discussed our teaching styles, personalities, and philosophies before entering the co-teaching partnership?
- Planned to use a variety of co-teaching models?
- Shared our preferred communication style?
- Discussed ways to apply research-based instructional teaching behaviors?
- Evaluated our co-teaching partnership?

ADDITIONAL RESOURCES ■

Books

Cramer, S. F. *The special educator's guide to collaboration.* Thousand Oaks, CA: Corwin Press.

Friend, M., & Cook, L. (2007). *Interactions: Collaboration skills for school professionals.* Boston: Pearson Education.

Murawski, W. W. (2003). *Co-teaching in the inclusive classroom: Working together to help all your students find success.* Medina, WA: Institute for Educational Development.

Villa, R. A., Thousand, J. S., & Nevin, A. I. (2004). *A guide to co-teaching.* Thousand Oaks, CA: Corwin Press.

Articles

Dieker, L. A., & Barnett, C. A. (1996). Effective co-teaching. *Teaching Exceptional Children, 29*(1), 5–7.

Fennick, E. (2001). Co teaching: An inclusive curriculum for transition. *Teaching Exceptional Children, 33*(6), 60–66.

Gately, S. E., & Gately, F. J. (2001). Understanding co-teaching components. *Teaching Exceptional Children, 33*(4), 40–47.

Murawski, W. M., & Dieker, L. A. (2004). Tips and strategies for co-teaching at the secondary level. *Teaching Exceptional Children, 36*(5), 52–58.

Murawski, W. M., & Dieker, L. A. (2008). Fifty ways to keep your co-teacher: Strategies for before, during, and after co-teaching. *Teaching Exceptional Children, 40*(4), 40–48.

Schumm, J., Vaughn, S., & Harris, J. (1997). Pyramid power for collaborative planning. *Teaching Exceptional Children, 29*(6), 62–66.

Vaughn, S., Schumm, J., & Arguelles, M. (1997). The ABCDEs of co-teaching. *Teaching Exceptional Children, 30*(2), 4–10.

3
Teaching So They Understand

Co-Teaching With Big Ideas

Mrs. Jung (general education social studies teacher) and Mrs. Jamal (special education teacher) have been assigned to co-teach a diverse seventh-grade social studies class in an inner-city setting that includes five students with IEPs, three students with attention deficit hyperactivity disorder (ADHD) who have 504 plans, two students who are English-language learners, and several other students who receive free or reduced lunch.

The textbook is written at a high school level that challenges all students but especially those with limited vocabulary and reading skills. Also, while both co-teachers are experienced, neither has co-teaching experience, nor did they receive professional development to prepare them for co-teaching. Further, the teachers do not have a common planning time, their classrooms are not in close proximity, and neither has a firm idea of how they are supposed to work together.

Because Mrs. Jamal teaches in another wing immediately before the co-taught class, she frequently arrives several minutes after the bell rings. This angers Mrs. Jung, who starts class by herself. Not wishing to distract students, Mrs. Jamal sits at the back of the room, and she frequently redirects students, helps them read, retypes class notes, helps students record assignments in planners, and develops study guides for upcoming tests. She helps students study notes during their resource period with her.

Although Mrs. Jamal provides much support for students, she is frustrated because she feels like an assistant rather than a co-teacher. She is constantly reactive rather than proactive. She never knows what is coming next. She knows that students have great difficulty remembering dates, new vocabulary, and names and that they seldom pass tests because of the amount of information they are expected to learn and remember. Further, they promptly forget memorized facts. Students also are not completing textbook-based homework assignments, probably due to the textbook readability level. Even when the book is put on audiotape, they do not understand the material because of unusual vocabulary and complex sentence structure.

Mrs. Jamal thought she should order books at students' reading levels that contain important content and design homework and practice sheets reviewing *critical information, but she does not know what information is critical and which information is less important. Because she is not the content area expert, Mrs. Jamal asked Mrs. Jung which information was the most important. In frustration, Mrs. Jung handed her the 643-page teacher's manual, 520-page textbook, 15-page district critical content, and 145-page supplemental workbook. Mrs. Jung said, "This is what I am supposed to cover this year!" Mrs. Jamal stared at the stack of books and was overwhelmed. She did not know where to begin.*

This team in a nutshell:

Grade level: 7

Classroom Contextual Factors: Diverse general education classroom

Subject: Social studies

Co-teaching stage: Beginning

Interpersonal issue: Anger surrounding late arrival for class; anger about not feeling like a co-teacher

Instructional challenges: Too much material and books too difficult

---

THE BIG IDEA   ■

The situation faced by the co-teachers in this scenario is typical of what many teachers all over the country at every grade level in all academic areas may be facing. Textbooks are difficult. Classrooms contain increased diversity. In some cases, classes contain a spread of five years in skill levels, yet teachers must ensure that all students meet state and local standards. Students are assessed on these standards, so teachers feel they must cover everything.

Attempting to meet the needs of all students and cover content pulls teachers in a thousand different directions. Instruction often becomes scattered as teachers race to cover the curriculum. In this race, teachers often use the textbook as the curriculum, hoping that by going through all the pages, they have covered the information and have at least exposed students to critical facts. However, such a coverage-oriented approach actually defeats its own aims. Teaching through exposure misses the students NCLB mandates educators to target.

To avoid this trap, teachers can design instruction around big ideas. A *big idea* is a concept, theme, or issue that gives meaning and connection to discrete facts and skills (Wiggins & McTighe, 2005). A big idea is the hub that holds content together. This chapter focuses on how to design instruction around big ideas so as to facilitate learning for all students.

After reading this chapter, you will be able to do the following:

- Describe the difficulty with using the textbook as the main or only curriculum source for content-area classes.
- Provide a rationale for designing instruction around big ideas.
- Describe how to craft big ideas and core questions for a course.
- Use big ideas and core questions to differentiate instruction and assessment for diverse learners.
- Explain the response-to-affect communication tool.

■ A RATIONALE FOR USING BIG IDEAS

American education presents two opposing forces with teachers caught in the middle: on one hand is the curriculum (often equated with the textbook), and on the other hand are the learning needs of an increasingly diverse body of students. Both forces provide a solid rationale for using big ideas.

First, in the United States, many teachers rely on the textbook as the major vehicle of information. When teachers say they have to cover the curriculum, they often mean they have to get through the textbook. The problem is that many textbooks contain too much information covered in too little depth using too high a level of language sophistication and not enough practice to ensure mastery. Teachers cannot possibly cover all the material established by textbook publishers. Our textbook-based curriculum has been described as being a mile wide and an inch deep. As a result, students are overstuffed and undernourished (Dempster, 1993). Using district-chosen textbooks as their curricula, teachers stuff a lot of information into students by getting through the textbooks. The result is that students are undernourished educationally. That is, they really do not learn anything in depth. Only the highest-performing students and those with a considerable amount of subject background knowledge are able to learn, understand, and apply material to which they are merely exposed (Coyne, Kame'enui, & Carnine, 2007).

The other challenge—and reason for teaching big ideas—is increased diversity in our classrooms. The demographics of the American classroom are changing dramatically. Students are increasingly diverse in language ability, background knowledge, and cognitive and sociological experiences. These factors place students at risk of academic failure.

Typically, most students considered at risk do not have the language sophistication to profit from traditional classroom instruction. They are unable to sift through information in textbooks or lectures to separate critical from noncritical concepts. Further, they do not spontaneously organize unfamiliar information, so they have difficulty remembering bits of information. Such students may remember some facts for upcoming tests, but they are unable to organize these facts for long-term memory storage. When teachers present a lot of information, most students, especially learners considered at risk, have difficulty learning the material well. When teachers present too much information, they often actually interfere with effective learning.

In short, because of the changing learning needs of students, teachers can no longer rely on the traditional approach of covering the curriculum. They can no longer depend on advancing through the textbook, because, quite simply, many students in diverse classrooms do not learn that way.

■ WHAT: THE DESIGN

If teachers can no longer rely on advancing through the textbook as an effective instructional strategy, what can they use as the basis of their instruction to ensure that all students learn the material? The answer lies in rethinking the design. Rather than basing the design of the course on the textbook, rethink the design. Start with the end in mind and design instruction backward (Wiggins & McTighe, 2005). Rather than focusing on weekly or daily lesson objectives, shift the focus backward to the end result. Ask these two important questions:

1. What are the central and organizing ideas I want all students to remember at the end of this course?
2. What evidence proves that students have learned these ideas?

To use this design effectively, start well before you walk into the classroom. Think of the course as a whole, rather than individual units, and ask yourself, "What are the 'big ideas'?"

This design process includes the following seven steps:

1. Read through state and district standards to formulate a few big ideas.
2. Write big ideas as course core questions.
3. Translate core questions into kid-friendly language.
4. Create a graphic organizer to visually represent
   a. big ideas and course questions and
   b. course units of study.
5. Tell students the big idea and display the visual.
6. Determine how students will provide evidence of learning core material.
7. Refer to big ideas daily as you teach.

Step 1: Select Big Ideas

While the concept of big ideas may appear simple, developing them is not easy. Teachers begin the process by creating the framework around which the course is organized. The first step to determine big ideas is to read through district standards or critical content for your subject area. As you read through this material and consider the course content, ask yourself these questions:

- What information, concepts, or ideas are critical for students to remember at the end of this course?
- Why should students learn this material?
- How does the material relate to students' lives now, and of what use will the information be to them in the future?
- What are the ideas and concepts that go beyond this course that have implications for broader issues that students must face?
- What are the central or big ideas that tie all this information together?

After you have considered the questions relative to your content area, formulate a few statements that represent big ideas for your course. For example, the big idea in social studies might be that a culture can be analyzed and compared by looking at its history, government, economic structure, geographic features, and intricacies of its society. In beginning reading, the big idea could be that understanding the sound structure of language and the alphabetic principal are components of reading. The big idea in writing instruction might be that writing goes through stages of planning, drafting, editing, and revising. The big idea in language arts might be that text structure can be used as a guide for reading and writing. The big idea in literature might be that authors use a variety of formats and literary techniques to draw readers into thinking deeply about important issues. Forming the big idea helps you remain focused as you move to the next step.

Step 2: Design Central Questions

Use the big idea and your district's critical content to guide you in reworking state and district standards into questions. Formulate questions rather than statements or concepts, so that students consider answers as they progress through the course. These questions must be broad enough that they can be revisited and reconsidered frequently, even daily, and they should be worded to stimulate conversation rather than elicit merely a one-word answer (Lenz, Schumaker, Deshler, & Bulgren, 1999). These questions form the central organizing framework of the course. Students should be able to use these questions to think deeply about course material and to tie material from each unit together. In helping you formulate questions, Lenz et al. recommends starting with the word *what* or *how*. Figure 3.1 provides additional examples of big ideas and central questions.

Step 3: Translate Central Questions Into "Kid-Friendly Language"

Next, translate central questions into language that students understand. For example, in our opening scenario, Mrs. Jung and Mrs. Jamal are teaching a seventh-grade social studies class. One big idea from their class may be this: cultures from prehistoric times through the Middle Ages can be analyzed and compared by looking at their histories, governments, economic structures, geographic features, and intricacies of their societies.

The translation of the central questions into student friendly language might be as follows:

Teacher Talk	Student-Friendly Language Translation
1. What were the interactions among people, places, and the environment?	1. *How does where this group of people lived affect how they lived?*
2. How do art and religion help us understand this culture?	2. A. *What do the art forms of this group of people tell us about them?* B. *What do the religious beliefs and practices of this group of people tell us about them?*
3. What technological advances did this culture contribute?	3. *What important discoveries did this group of people make?*
4. How did this culture organize to produce, distribute, and consume goods and services?	4. *How did this group of people get what they needed to live?*
5. How did these various cultures and times affect each other and our lives today?	5. *How does this culture affect us today?*
6. How did each culture create and change the structure of power, authority, and governance?	6. *Who was in charge and how did they get to be in power? How were they organized?*
7. What contributed to the rise and fall of each culture?	7. *How did each culture get power and stay in power, and what caused it to lose power?*

Figure 3.1   Examples of Core Questions From Various Grade Levels and Curricular Areas

Elementary Example: Reading and Language Arts

Big idea: By understanding the organizational features of language, you will be able to read, write, listen, and speak with greater understanding.

Core Questions:

How does the structure of this word help you to read and spell it and know what it means?

How do sentences differ?

What is the structure of this paragraph?

How do texts differ?

How does the text structure help your reading and understanding?

How do you know when you do not understand what you are reading?

What do you do when you do not understand what you are reading?

How do stories about other places and times affect you?

How do writers express their thoughts and feelings?

How is written language different from spoken language?

High School Civic Example

Big idea: We can become responsible citizens by studying how our state and federal governments are organized and how we participate in a world community.

Core Questions:

What purpose should government serve?

What is the political system of the United States, and how has it developed?

What events significantly influenced the development of our political system?

What values and principles are basic to the American political system?

How have individuals and religious and other interest groups influenced the political systems of our state, our country, and other countries?

What are the responsibilities of citizenship?

How can citizens take part in political life?

How are other countries organized politically?

How has the United States influenced other nations, and how have other nations influenced American politics and society?

What are the relationships and tensions among countries in the international arena?

Determining the big idea and formulating core questions are essential, because they provide the instructional focus and framework. Without this design feature, teaching becomes a rote activity of presenting facts. In contrast, with this design, Mrs. Jamal can select alternate reading materials and design activities to help students grasp big ideas and core questions.

Step 4: Design a Visual

Use one of the graphic organizer formats presented in Chapter 5 or design one of your own to represent core questions and units of study. Develop a graphic organizer that represents each unit of study and connects core questions. Remember that the purpose of this graphic organizer, such as the one shown in Figure 3.2, is to organize course content so that students can see how the parts are related.

Figure 3.2   Course Overview

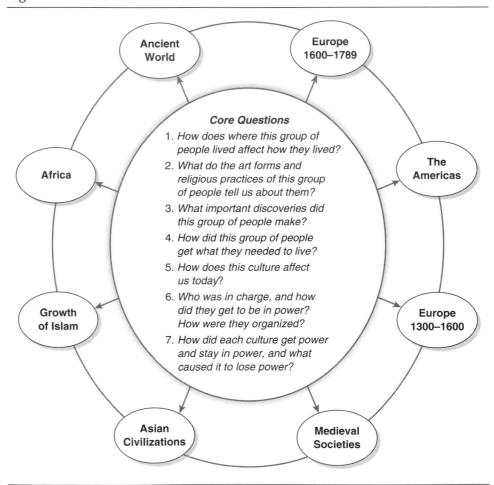

Step 5: Display and Use the Visual

Make the graphic organizer large enough to be seen by the entire class. One way to do this is by creating the organizer on standard-size paper, taking it to your local copy store, and requesting they enlarge it to poster size. The cost is minimal, usually under $5, but well worth the savings in time and energy. Another option, if you have the space, is to create a bulletin board, which remains up for the entire term, with core ideas in the center and units spreading out. As you proceed through the course, refer to the organizer often, even daily, to remind students of the core questions that help them organize material. By referring to the questions often, you provide the repeated practice learners need to understand and integrate content. In addition to the whole-class display, provide each student with a copy of the graphic organizer and tell the student where to keep it in his class notebook.

Step 6: Determine How Students Will Provide Evidence of Learning Core Material

As presented in Chapter 8, teachers can design various assessment tools to determine if students have learned course material. Decide ahead of time how students will provide evidence of their learning and include those assessment tools as part of the design. For example, Mrs. Jung and Mrs. Jamal could have students do the following as evidence of mastering core material:

1. Create a time line plotting each culture.
2. Compare and contrast two cultures visually or in essay format.
3. Draw a diagram of the rise and fall of a culture.
4. Draw a physical map of the culture, indicating basic land and water forms.

When designing evidence of learning tools, focus on core questions; everything you require of students should be directly linked to core questions. As an assistant superintendent directed her teachers, *"Ask yourself, is it cute, or does it count?"* (Sorrick, 2007, emphasis added). If every activity, homework assignment, worksheet, and test question contributes toward an understanding of core questions, you will be providing students with the essential practice they need for revisiting big ideas. When you assign a chapter to read or worksheet to complete, be sure you can explain its connection to core questions. In other words, tell students what they will learn by completing the activity.

Step 7: Be Explicit

Do not expect learners who are at risk to determine core questions by reading the textbook or listening to lectures. Typically, these learners need support extracting essential from nonessential information. You can be explicit in the following ways:

- Tell students essential information.
- Frequently remind them to review core questions.
- Refer back to core questions frequently.
- Prominently display core questions.
- Remind students which core question you are addressing in a particular lesson or activity.
- Remind them of the core question often during the lesson.

In other words, do not keep the essential information or core questions a secret.

You can also incorporate core questions into your opening teaching routine in the following ways:

- Tell students the core question you are addressing in a particular lesson, such as by saying, "Today we are going to begin the study of Ghana. We are going to start by looking at where Ghana is located. Look at our course core questions. The core question we are going to address today is Question #1. Everyone look at the course organizer chart." (Select a student volunteer to read the question.)

- Explain the rationale for learning the material by stating, "We study the location of a culture because location provides important information about how the culture existed. We can also learn how that culture affected or changed the land in which the people lived."
- Note how the material is connected to other course sections by stating, "We have studied other cultures. Look at the organizer to review the other cultures we have studied. We have also looked at their locations. Tell your partner something you remember about the locations of other cultures we have studied. Also tell your partner how the location affected the culture and how the culture changed the land. What did your partner tell you?"
- Explain how students will demonstrate their learning by noting, "When we have finished this part, you should be able to find Ghana on a map; draw a physical map of Ghana indicating major landforms, waterways, and longitude and latitude line; tell how the land affected the people; and write a short paragraph about the relationship between the people of Ghana and the land in which they lived."

■ TEACHER BEHAVIORS: USING THE STEPS

Mrs. Jamal and Mrs. Jung can use the seven steps as they jointly plan their course or a unit in the course. Here are our co-teachers in action, using these steps:

Strategy Steps	Co-Teachers' Response
1. Determine critical course content.	Independently, Mrs. Jamal and Mrs. Jung read through the district's critical content for this grade level. They developed and shared a statement of the big ideas during an initial planning session. Mrs. Jung outlined the eight units of the course in chronological order.
2. Design five to ten essential questions that capture the essence of the course.	Using state standards, the district's critical content, and Social Studies Content standards from the National Council of Social Studies (NCSS), both co-teachers developed eight questions they felt embodied course content. As they formulated each question, Mrs. Jung referred back to the content of the course to ensure each question was addressed in each unit.
3. Write the questions in kid-friendly language.	The co-teachers worded questions to promote student understanding.
4. Design a graphic organizer.	The co-teachers decided that the best graphic organizer to display the course was the "wheel," with the core questions in the center and units spreading out from the hub. They felt that the wheel graphic also functioned as a metaphor for the class, as the wheel was one of the important inventions of prehistoric humanity.
5. Refer to the organizer when planning, teaching, and assessing.	The co-teachers designed a bulletin board displaying the "wheel" organizer. In addition, each student was given a copy of the organizer for the social studies binder. The co-teachers

Strategy Steps	Co-Teachers' Response
	also kept a copy in their plan books. When planning lessons, they continually referred to the "hub" (core questions) to ensure that daily plans reflected and supported core questions. Mrs. Jamal used the wheel organizer to locate additional reading material at adjusted reading levels that supported core questions. By using core questions, Mrs. Jung was less dependent upon the textbook, but she had the freedom to use the book as appropriate.
6. Determine how students will provide evidence of learning critical content.	Having core questions to guide them, the co-teachers designed activities for learning and assessments based on varying student skill levels. For example, students with higher language and writing skills completed research and wrote a five-paragraph expository essay, while students who had difficulty with reading and writing wrote one paragraph. Mrs. Jamal assisted in making accommodations and modifications and teaching research and paragraph-writing skills.
7. Be explicit.	The co-teachers used this opening routine as a guide as they planned lessons. They addressed all four steps in each lesson to communicate with students, remain focused, and provide a similar learning experience for all students.
a. Tell the students what they are learning.	The co-teachers begin each class by setting an explicit purpose for each lesson, such as, "Class, today we are going to learn about how the people of Ghana got things they needed to survive. Look at your wheel organizer or look up at the bulletin board. On your dry erase boards [active learning], write the core question we will be investigating today."
b. Tell the students why they are learning it.	Establishing a reason students have to learn a particular topic is often difficult and requires much thought on the part of the co-teachers. An effective strategy to begin the conversation is to ask students why they think they are studying a certain topic. The co-teachers could ask: "Why are we learning about this? Why is this topic included in the state and district standards? How can we benefit from learning this?"
c. Tell the students how it is connected to the organizer.	The co-teachers always refer back to the wheel organizer to connect material to be learned to material that had been presented before. They could say: "We have studied other cultures and learned about how people got the things they needed. With your partner, talk about the other cultures we have studied and how those people got what they needed to survive. Who can tell the class what their partner told them?"
d. Tell the students how they will demonstrate they have learned the material.	The co-teachers indicate how students will be assessed on their learning. They could say: "When we have finished today's lesson, you are going to design a Venn diagram comparing two different cultures. One of the cultures will be Ghana, and the other culture will be your choice. Listen carefully and read with the goal to learn at least three different ways in which the people of Ghana obtained what they needed to survive."

■ BACK TO OUR TEAM

Mrs. Jamal, the special education teacher, felt she could be doing more to help students and her co-teacher. She felt she was more reactive by responding to students' needs on a minute-to-minute basis rather than being proactive by coplanning and coinstructing. In this situation, Mrs. Jamal could first respond to the underlying message her colleague is sending by using the response-to-affect technique.

This technique is appropriate in this situation, because before Mrs. Jamal can present the curricular issue, she must first acknowledge that she has understood her co-teacher's message. Obviously, Mrs. Jung is frustrated and overwhelmed, as noted by her behavior of stacking books on the table and using a loud voice. Mrs. Jamal can begin by indicating that she understands the emotion by validating her partner's feeling. Then, the team can move forward and address curricular issues such as teaching using big ideas.

Response to Affect

Looking at the stack of books on the table, Mrs. Jamal could say, "Wow, this really is a lot of material to get through. You must be frustrated and overwhelmed by all of these goals and standards and feeling pressure to cover them."

The Result

Mrs. Jung has been totally overwhelmed by the enormity of the challenge of covering the curriculum, and she felt relieved when Mrs. Jamal indicated she understood the situation and was willing to assist. In this example of co-teaching, the majority of the teamwork must be done outside of classroom. To be effective, though, co-teachers need common planning time. In this situation, which is typical of that of many co-teachers nationwide, teachers do not share a common planning time, so they find other times and ways to plan, reflect on the success of the lesson, rework the plan based on student needs, and determine the best method to deliver the next phase of the lesson. Without common planning time, co-teaching often becomes relegated to one teach, one follow. In that case, the co-teaching situation is less purposeful and does not become a powerful instructional tool.

Realizing the importance of making time to plan together, Mrs. Jamal and Mrs. Jung approached their administrator with their need. The administrator was a proponent of co-teaching who acknowledged the necessity of having a common planning time and was able to rework the schedule to create a daily coplanning time. The teachers also shared their need to have both co-teachers present at the beginning of class. The schedule change also allowed Mrs. Jamal to arrive on time. If scheduling would not allow Mrs. Jamal to begin on time, the co-teaching team could consider the options described in Chapter 2. With a different instructional perspective, a new schedule, and renewed energy, the two co-teachers begin to plan the next few days. They agree to use the seven-step process for remaining units. Until then, they agree to integrate components of the design system into daily lesson plans.

LESSON PLANS ■

Day 1

Anticipatory set: Mrs. Jamal welcomes students and begins by sharing the what, why, and how of today's lesson. She could say something like, "Today we are learning about culture. We will learn a definition of *culture*, what culture is and is not, and we will look at some examples of culture. Learning about culture is important, because its study tells us how people in different countries and times live and how they are similar and different from each other. We have already studied the culture of our state. Before you leave today, you will complete the guided notes on culture and determine examples of the current youth culture in the United States. Today we are studying the question: What does the culture of a people tell about what is important to its citizens?" This question is revealed on the whiteboard and appears on the guided notes and culture worksheet students will later complete. While Mrs. Jamal distributes the guided notes and culture worksheet, Mrs. Jung begins the PowerPoint presentation.

Instruction: Mrs. Jung presents a PowerPoint presentation on cultures, which includes big ideas from the text as well as supplemental information. The beginning of the presentation presents the definition of *culture*, components of culture, and what culture is and is not. Periodically, as is her routine, she pauses to ask students questions about the presentation and engages them in discussion. Mrs. Jamal verbally adds examples of culture, as well, as she circulates to ensure students are completing their guided notes. As she circulates, she observes errors students have made on their guided notes, and she clarifies the correct response through classwide guided questions.

Student practice activity: With partners, students complete the "Culture of the United States" worksheet that accompanied the text. Using the definition of *culture* and information from the PowerPoint presentation, student pairs brainstorm examples of contemporary U.S. youth culture in various categories, such as art, religion, music, communications, technologies, etc. Both co-teachers circulate to offer assistance and to challenge early finishers to add additional examples to their sheet.

Class discussion: As groups finish, Mrs. Jung engages the class in a discussion about their examples, and various groups share examples from their sheets. As groups share, Mrs. Jamal takes notes on the overhead. Both co-teachers offer additional stimulating questions about youth culture to help students think about the youth culture from different geographical areas, ethnicities, and historical periods. They also direct the discussion back to the guiding question for the day.

Closure: Before students are dismissed, Mrs. Jamal asks each student to respond to the question of the day. Students write no more than three sentences on the question: What does the culture of a today's youth in the United States tell about what is important to them? As students finish their independent activity and submit their completed worksheets, they are dismissed.

Day 2

Anticipatory set: Mrs. Jamal welcomes students and begins by sharing the what, why, and how of today's lesson. She could say something like,

"Today we are continuing our study on culture. We will look at the culture of a country we are studying, which is Ghana. Remember, knowing the culture of a country helps us understand and appreciate the people and the way they live. Yesterday, we learned about culture and the youth culture in the United States. Today, you will research one aspect of Ghana's culture in depth, and tomorrow, your group will teach the class what you have learned. You will submit this 'Ghana Culture Sheet' as evidence of your learning. We are continuing to address our critical question: What does the culture of a people tell about what is important to its citizens? Be thinking about that question as you complete your research."

Review: Both co-teachers ask review questions to assess what students remember about culture, components of culture, and how culture reflects the values of the people.

Instruction: Mrs. Jamal presents the activity. In predetermined groups of three, students will study one aspect of Ghana's culture. The teachers have already gathered many materials for each group, such as supplemental books, Web sites, photocopied textbook pages, and video clips. Mrs. Jung shows the "Ghana Culture Sheet" on the overhead and explains how to complete the sheet. She also emphasizes that today, each group of three will research one aspect of contemporary Ghana culture, and over the next two days, groups will present their findings to the class though short presentations. She also indicates how groups will be evaluated by showing and distributing the "Ghana Culture Presentation Rubric."

Group work: Students gather in groups and study their assigned culture. Both co-teachers circulate to help students process information and decide their final presentation formats, such as a poster or a role-play. Some students work at the computers, others go to the library, and some work in the hall; most remain in the classroom.

Closure: About five minutes before the bell, both co-teachers prepare for closure by directing students to return materials, return to their seats, and prepare to write summaries of what they learned about Ghana's culture and how they will teach that to the class tomorrow. After students complete this brief writing activity, they are dismissed.

Day 3 and Day 4

Anticipatory set: Mrs. Jung welcomes students and sets the learning agenda for the day. She reminds students of the question of the week. She indicates that they will write a one- to two-sentence response after each group presentation: What did you learn about the people of Ghana from this presentation?

Student practice: Student groups are given ten minutes to practice or rehearse their presentation.

Group presentations: Through volunteering or picking numbers out of a box, five student groups present their cultural summaries. Some groups present a poster, others complete a role-play, others present a mini TV talk show presentation, etc. As groups present, both co-teachers independently score the rubric. After each presentation, the class is allowed to ask questions to members of the performing group (or the co-teachers) before they write their response to the question.

BIG IDEAS AND CO-TEACHING MODELS ◾

In the past, our co-teaching team primarily used the one-teach, one-support model. However, these teachers could use the other co-teaching models, as well.

- *One teach, one observe:* This format could be used if one teacher wanted feedback on her teaching techniques. Mrs. Jamal may want feedback on her effectiveness teaching a larger group of students. While she presents the lesson, Mrs. Jung could observe certain teaching behaviors and their effects on students. Perhaps Mrs. Jamal is concerned about students' off-task behavior during the lecture part of the lesson. Mrs. Jung could observe students and provide feedback to Mrs. Jamal. Co-teachers could switch roles, with one teaching and the other observing.
- *One teach, one drift:* As one teacher presents the lesson, the other teacher could circulate around the room, observe how students respond, and assist as needed. This is the role Mrs. Jamal had before the team began planning together. Both teachers need to assume both the teacher and drifter roles for students to understand teacher parity.
- *Parallel teaching:* Dividing the class in half and having each teacher present the same lesson to her half could be used when introducing a topic that both teachers feel comfortable teaching. This model can also be used to multiply the impact of instruction. For example, Mrs. Jamal could have her students learn two cultures, Mrs. Jung could have her students study two different cultures, and students could come together in pairs to teach each other about their chosen cultures.
- *Alternate teaching:* Co-teachers may use this format to provide additional instruction for a student who had been absent. One teacher would teach the class, while the other reteaches a smaller group. Teachers could also use this model to differentiate instruction. For example, one teacher could teach paragraph writing or research skills to a smaller group, while the other teacher provides instruction in essay writing.
- *Station teaching:* As a review activity, teachers could design mini station activities that reconnect students to the core questions of the unit. In small groups, students circulate among the stations to complete purposeful activities.
- *Team teaching:* During their planning session, co-teachers decide upon the lesson goals and agree to teach the lesson jointly. They may decide who takes the lead in certain parts of the lesson, with each teacher feeling free to add additional examples or information as necessary.

SUMMARY ◾

This chapter presented a rationale and a model for determining big ideas and core questions for a course. This instructional approach contrasts with the traditional method of covering facts. When co-teachers use the steps described in this chapter, both can effectively deliver instruction to a diverse group of learners. The major components of this approach include the following seven steps:

1. Determine the critical content of the course.

2. Design five to ten essential questions that capture the essence of the course.

3. Write the questions in kid-friendly language.

4. Design a graphic organizer.

5. Refer to the organizer when planning, teaching, and assessing.

6. Determine how students will provide evidence of learning critical content.

7. Be explicit by telling students (a) what they are learning, (b) the rationale for learning the material, (c) how the material is connected, and (d) how they will demonstrate that they have learned the material.

The chapter emphasized the importance of acknowledging and validating your co-teacher's concerns and frustrations by using a response-to-affect statement. This communication tool is especially appropriate when co-teachers want to empathize and connect emotionally with their teaching partners. Often, validating your partner's emotion is needed before co-planning and co-teaching can begin. The chapter also mentioned the importance of administrator assistance, especially when scheduling issues conflict with successful co-teaching.

■ REFLECTIONS TO APPLICATION

As co-teachers, have we . . .

- Selected instructional materials representing various reading levels?
- Discussed the importance of teaching big ideas?
- Crafted the big ideas and core questions for our class?
- Implemented the seven steps of the design process to differentiate instruction and assessment?

■ ADDITIONAL RESOURCES

Books

Barell, J. (2007). *Problem-based learning.* Thousand Oaks, CA: Corwin Press.

Bulgren, J. A., Schumaker, J. B., & Deshler, D. D. (1993). *The content enhancement series: The concept mastery routine.* Lawrence, KS: Edge Enterprises.

Lenz, B. K., Bulgren, J. A., Schumaker, J. B., Deshler, D. D., & Boudah, D. A. (1994). *The content enhancement series: The unit organizer routine.* Lawrence, KS: Edge Enterprises.

McTighe, J., & Wiggins, G. (2004). *Understanding by design: Professional development workbook.* Alexandria, VA: Association for Supervision and Curriculum Development.

Articles

Burns, M. (2004). 10 big math ideas. *Instructor, 113*(7), 16–20.

Carnine, D., & Bean, R. (1994). Social studies: Educational tools for diverse learners. *School Psychology Review, 23*(3), 428, 442.

Edwards, T. G. (2000). Some big ideas of algebra in the middle school. *Mathematics Teaching in the Middle School, 6,* 26–31.

Ellis, E. S. (1997). Watering up the curriculum for adolescents with learning disabilities. *Remedial and Special Education, 18,* 326–346.

Ellis, E. S., Farmer, T., & Newman, J. (2005). Big ideas about teaching the big ideas. *Teaching Exceptional Children, 38*(1), 34 40.

Grossen, B., Caros, J., Carnine, D., Davis, B., Deshler, D., Schumaker, J., Bulgren, J., et al. (2002). Big ideas (plus a little effort) produce big results. *Teaching Exceptional Children, 34*(4), 70–73.

Simmons, D. C., & Kame'enui, E. J. (1996). A focus on curriculum design: When children fail. *Focus on Exceptional Children, 28*(7), 1–16.

Twyman, T., Ketterlin-Geller, L. R., McCoy., J. D., & Tindal, G. (2003). Effects of concept-based instruction on an English language learner in a rural school: A descriptive case study. *Bilingual Research, 27*(2), 259–274.

Woodbury, S. (2000). Teaching toward the big ideas of algebra. *Mathematics Teaching in the Middle School, 6*(4), 226–231.

Web Sites

The University of Oregon has a Web site on the big ideas of beginning reading: http://reading.uoregon.edu/big_ideas/trial_bi_index.php.

The standards for English can be obtained from the National Council of Teachers of English: www.ncte.org/about/over/standards/110846.htm.

The standards for mathematics can be obtained from the National Council of Teachers of Mathematics: http://standards.nctm.org/document/appendix/numb.htm.

The standards for social studies can be obtained from the National Council for the Social Studies: www.ncss.org/standards/.

The standards for science can be obtained from the National Science Teachers Association: www.nsta.org/publications/nses.aspx.

4

Teaching So They Remember

Co-Teaching With Mnemonics

Fifth-grade co-teachers Mr. McClusky (general educator) and Miss Evans (special educator) are concluding their social studies unit on their home state, Iowa. Mr. McClusky, who has been teaching for seven years, describes himself as a traditional teacher—he often uses discussion and independent seatwork in his class. This is Miss Evans's second year of teaching special education but her first year at McGregor Elementary School. Miss Evans describes herself as a pragmatist—she uses whatever method works for her students. This team has only been co-teaching for three weeks, the length of this unit. So far, they have used the one-teach, one-drift and one-teach, one-observe models, and Miss Evans has consistently assumed the passive instructional role. These models have been appropriate for teaching this unit, but Miss Evans would like to contribute more meaningfully to the co-teaching situation. However, she is uncomfortable confronting others—especially her senior teaching partner. At the same time, both teachers have discovered that students in this diverse class have not been retaining factual information from this unit of study; consequently, student quiz scores have been poor.

This team in a nutshell:

Grade level: 5

Classroom contextual factors: Diverse classroom demographics

Subject: Social studies

Co-teaching stage: Beginning

Interpersonal issue: Afraid to confront

Instructional challenge: Students are not retaining information

MNEMONICS   ■

A jingle, a rhyme, a phrase, a song, or a visual—all of these can be mnemonics. A mnemonic is any devise that aids memorization. Mnemonics are artificial aids imposed on the curriculum to help students recall factual information, such as names, dates, figures, or lists. Recall some of your favorite TV commercials—you probably remember words to the jingle, melody, or rhyme. You might even be able to visualize the commercial, as well as your surroundings when you first saw and heard it. Mnemonics can be powerful learning tools.

This chapter focuses on using mnemonics in co-taught classrooms. You will learn the importance of mnemonics and effective strategies for teaching them. After reading this chapter, you will be able to do the following:

- Define *mnemonics* and provide examples of mnemonics.
- Provide a rationale for using mnemonics in your classroom.
- Describe several specific mnemonic strategies.
- Explain ways to incorporate mnemonics in co-taught classrooms.
- Describe one way to confront your co-teacher effectively, even when you dislike confrontation.

A RATIONALE FOR USING MNEMONICS   ■

Why should teachers infuse mnemonic instruction into their classrooms? First, mnemonics have a great track record. This is especially important considering the mandate for using research-based practices. In their meta-analysis of the most popular instructional methods used in special education, researchers Lloyd, Forness, and Kavale (1998) discovered that mnemonics produced the most significant academic gains for students with disabilities. Mnemonics were more powerful than direct instruction, reading comprehension strategies, behavior modification, early intervention, or even reducing class size. However, mnemonics—like other learning tools—need to be taught explicitly to some students. Although many students can develop their own mnemonics for remembering items for an upcoming test or quiz, other students in diverse classrooms typically need considerable support—at least initially—in developing their own mnemonics.

Second, mnemonics help students compensate for some of their learning issues. Many students in diverse classrooms have language, memory, or other information-processing issues that interfere with learning. Mnemonics provide a strategy that compensates for these learning challenges. Instead of relying on memory for remembering a list of six items for an upcoming exam, for example, students could just remember a key word, phrase, sentence, or picture. Similarly, many students with—or without—disabilities have poor study skills. These students may be overwhelmed by the amount of information presented to them. Mnemonics provide an important support for organizing and retaining large amounts of information. Mnemonic instruction is especially appropriate for students who have IEP study skills goals and objectives.

A third reason for considering mnemonic instruction is that teachers emphasize learning factual information. Although class discussions and activities may activate higher thinking levels, many content area exam questions are at the knowledge or factual level. Consequently, it is not unusual for middle or high school students in inclusion content area classes to be required to display mastery of 60 to 80 facts per test (Deshler & Schumaker, 2006). In this age of accountability, students are taking more tests and being held accountable for more information. Mnemonics can be used at any grade level in any subject and in special education, general education, or co-taught classrooms with teachers like Mr. McClusky and Miss Evans.

DIFFERENT TYPES OF MNEMONICS

Students can learn to use a variety of different types of mnemonics as they review and study for tests. The two main categories of mnemonics are acronyms (words, phrases, rhymes, jingles, and sentences) and visuals (pictures, illustrations, and icons). Here are some examples of each:

Acronyms

- *Rhymes: When two vowels go walking, the first does the talking.*
- *Catch phrase: In 1492, Columbus sailed the ocean blue.*
- *Spelling acronym:* To help students remember the letters in spelling the word *because,* teach this sentence: *Big elephants can always understand small elephants.*
- *List order acronym:* Remember the names of the Great Lakes with the word **Homes** (**H**uron, **O**ntario, **M**ichigan, **E**rie, **S**uperior).
- *Sentence or phrase:* Teach the order of taxonomy in biology with this sentence: *Kids prefer cheese over fried green spinach* (**k**ingdom, **p**hylum, **c**lass, **o**rder, **f**amily, **g**enus, and **s**pecies). Also, remember the order of steps in an algebra problem with this sentence: *Please excuse my dear Aunt Sally* (**p**arenthesis, **e**xponents, **m**ultiplication, **d**ivision, **a**ddition, **s**ubtraction).

Visuals

- *Illustration:* Add an illustration to any of the above acronyms to increase their power and effectiveness. For example, provide a picture of two elephants to help students remember the spelling acronym for the word *because.*
- *Visualization:* Students close their eyes and mentally picture the items in the list, often incorporating the items into a story.
- *Snapshot strategy:* Students are provided an illustration or drawing that includes everything they need to remember about a particular concept. Students study this picture to recall the items associated with the concept.
- *The key word strategy:* Students draw a vocabulary word in an interactive image. This visual helps them remember the word better.

THE FIRST-LETTER MNEMONIC STRATEGY ■

One proven mnemonic strategy that can be used in a variety of classrooms is the FIRST-letter mnemonic strategy (Nagel, Schumaker, & Deshler, 1986). This strategy uses acronyms and sentences to help students remember items in a list for an upcoming exam. Each step of the strategy begins with one of the letters *F, I, R, S,* or *T.* These steps are shown in Figure 4.1 and explained below.

Often, students must remember items in a list taken from the text, a teacher's presentation, a video, or a Web site. Sometimes, the first letters of the items in that sequence make a word. If so, students can use the *F* (Form a word) step of the FIRST strategy. For example, as shown in Figure 4.1, when Mr. McClusky presented an introductory PowerPoint presentation, one of his slides indicated Iowa's capitol, Des Moines; state tree, Oak; and state bird, Eastern goldfinch.

If students needed to remember these items, they could remember the word *doe,* which would help them retrieve the necessary information. In this example, students would not have to change the order of the items on the list. Remembering *doe* helps them retrieve factual information for the quiz.

Other times, the first letters of words on the list do not make a word unless an additional letter is added. As shown in Figure 4.1, when students read about Iowa, they learned that Iowa leads the nation in the production

Figure 4.1   Steps and Examples of the FIRST-Letter Mnemonic Strategy

---

1. Form a word.

Involves: Making a word from the first letter of items in a list

Example: **D**es Moines, **o**ak, and **E**astern goldfinch become DOE.

2. Insert a letter (or letters).

Involves: Inserting a letter or letters to make a word while maintaining the order of items

Example: **P**ork, **e**ggs, and **s**oybeans become PIES (letter *I* inserted).

3. Rearrange the letters.

Involves: Rearranging the letters to make a word when order is not important

Example: **M**aytag, **R**ockwell, and **A**mana become ARM.

4. Shape a sentence.

Involves: Making a sentence using the first letters of the list items

Example: **R**eed, **C**arson, **W**ood, **H**oover, and **M**iller become *Real cows will have milk.*

5. Try different combinations.

Involves: Using two or more of the previous steps to make a mnemonic

Example: **B**eaconsfield, **L**eRoy, **P**ioneer, and **M**illville become *Paula likes blueberry muffins* (letters rearranged *and* a sentence formed).

---

of **p**ork, **e**ggs, and **s**oybeans—but *pes* does not make a word. To help remember these items, students could insert a letter, such as *i*, to the list to make the word *pies*. They would need to remember that the letter *i* was added as the filler letter. If students add a letter to make a word for their mnemonic, they should maintain the original letter sequence (e.g., *p-e-s*) of the items in the list.

Sometimes order is not important, so students can rearrange items on the list, so that they can use the first letters of the items to construct a word. For example, the teacher may be interested in having students remember that three important companies in Iowa include **M**aytag, **R**ockwell, and **A**mana. Rearranging the first letters of these industries produces the mnemonic *Arm*. Teachers need to communicate to students whether or not order is important for their lists.

The next step of the FIRST strategy is to shape a sentence. This step is appropriate when the previous steps do not work, often because items in the list do not contain vowels. In this step, students develop a sentence with the first letters of the items in the list. For example, if Mr. McClusky and Miss Evans want students to remember famous people from Iowa, they could provide this list: Donna **R**eed, Johnny **C**arson, Grant **W**ood, Herbert **H**oover, and Glenn **M**iller. Looking just at last names, we have the letters *R, C, W, H,* and *M*. A shape-a-sentence mnemonic for remembering these letters and names could be *Real cows will have milk*. Sentences should make sense and be grammatically correct. Often, students remember the mnemonic better when they develop their own sentences. They can also develop a visual or illustration to reinforce further their memory for their sentence.

The final step of the FIRST strategy is to try different combinations of the previous steps. This is a flexible step that is found in most strategies. In this step, to develop a mnemonic, the student might rearrange the letters and shape a sentence or, alternatively, insert a letter and shape a sentence. Because this step combines two or more steps of the strategy and is, therefore, more complex, typically students use this step only after they have exhausted previous steps. If students were learning the smallest towns in Iowa (**B**eaconsfield, **L**eRoy, **P**ioneer, and **M**illville) and were unsuccessful developing a mnemonic using the first four steps of the FIRST-letter mnemonic strategy, they could combine two steps, for example by rearranging the letters (because order is not important in this case) and shaping a sentence to form the mnemonic: *Paula likes blueberry muffins.*

■ THE KEY WORD STRATEGY

In addition to acronyms and sentences, as used in the FIRST-letter mnemonic strategy, visuals can be mnemonics. A well-known visual mnemonic is the key word strategy (Mastropieri & Scruggs, 1998), which helps students remember concepts and vocabulary words. This method can be used in a wide range of curricular subjects in diverse classrooms. It involves these three steps:

1. Students think of a key word. This key word must be acoustically similar to the vocabulary word, familiar to them, and an easily pictured, concrete term. For example, assume that for an upcoming quiz in social studies, students need to remember the following:

> *negotiate* means when groups talk with each other about how to solve a problem

They develop the key phrase *knees go straight*. This fits the criteria, because *knees go straight* is acoustically similar to *negotiate*, students understand this phrase, and they can draw a picture of a person's knees being straight (not bending).

> Vocabulary word or concept: *Negotiate*

> Key word/phrase: *Knees go straight.*

2. Students relate their key word to the vocabulary word or concept in an interactive image, picture, or sentence. In this step, students draw a picture of both of these words or phrases interacting. Therefore, students would picture groups of people, with their knees straight, talking with each other about solving a problem. Students might develop these pictures on note cards or flash cards, so they can quiz themselves later, or they might develop several of these on one page as a vocabulary list.

3. When students need to retrieve the vocabulary definition or concept, they think of the key word, the picture, and the action in the picture. After studying and reviewing for the upcoming social studies vocabulary quiz, when the term *negotiate* appears on the quiz, teachers remind students to (a) remember the key phrase, (b) recall the interactive image, and (c) retrieve the definition embedded in the interactive image. A student's self-talk might go like this: "Hmmm, negotiate. The key phrase was 'knees go straight.' I drew a picture of groups of people who could not sit down—they had to keep their knees straight while solving their problem. I remember now that *negotiate* refers to groups talking with each other to solve a problem."

THE SNAPSHOT METHOD   ■

Another powerful visual mnemonic strategy is the snapshot method. This method also uses a drawing or illustration to help students remember key information. By themselves, in groups, or with a teacher, students draw a picture that includes all the items on their list they need to remember. Then they use this drawing as a study tool. For example, as shown in Figure 4.2, for their state exam, students needed to remember the six inventions that enabled settlement of the western United States.

All six items (six-shooter, windmill, sod house, locomotive, steel plow, and barbed wire) are drawn in one illustration. This "snapshot" illustration serves as a visual mnemonic for students as they study. When students need to retrieve the information, they think of the six items drawn in their picture.

Figure 4.2   Snapshot Method

Information to be learned: The six inventions that enabled the settlement of the western United States

Answer:

- Six-shooter
- Windmill
- Sod house
- Locomotive
- Steel plow
- Barbed wire

Method: Draw all six items in one picture, diagram, or illustration for students to study. Students study (or draw) the picture and then recall the items in the picture for the upcoming test or quiz.

Source: Schumaker, J. B., Bulgren, J. A., Deshler, D. D., & Lenz, B. K. (1998). *The recall enhancement routine.* Lawrence, KS: University of Kansas.

■ THE VISUALIZATION METHOD

The visualization method is another example of a visual mnemonic, but in this method, students integrate visuals into a story. The story serves as a tool for remembering items. For example, assume that students in Mr. McClusky and Miss Evan's class wanted to remember these items about Iowa: *pigs, corn, goldfinch, oak, eggs, soybeans, Maytag, Rockwell, Amana.* They could make their drawing of each item (as explained in the snapshot method), but they could also link these items together in a story, such as this one:

> One day, as I was looking in my *Amana* refrigerator for some *eggs,* I heard the song of a *goldfinch* in my *oak* tree. I looked out the window and saw my neighbor, who works at *Rockwell,* feeding *corn* and *soybeans* to some *pigs.* I thought about this as I went to retrieve laundry out of my *Maytag* washing machine.

■ TEACHER BEHAVIORS

Regardless of the mnemonic method being taught to students, we offer these suggestions:

- Do not assume that all students in diverse classrooms will naturally think of using mnemonics when attempting to remember items for an upcoming exam. Therefore, explicitly teach students about mnemonics, their value, and specific situations in which to use them. Cues such as, "This would be a good time to use a mnemonic," serve as an important auditory reminder for students.

- Although mnemonics are typically used to help students remember factual information and details, show students how mnemonics can also help them remember big ideas from their units of study.
- When students have mastered the steps of the mnemonic strategy, encourage them to develop their own mnemonics rather than relying on the teacher's mnemonic. Students from diverse cultures may want to use a word from their native language.
- Discuss using mnemonics across the curriculum, so students see application in math, music, English, and various content areas.
- Introduce a variety of mnemonic structures, so students experience many different types. Encourage them to use the mnemonic that works best for them. Some students learn through visual methods and will use the visual examples, while others find acronyms more to their liking.
- Encourage students to share their mnemonics with each other as a cooperative learning activity or test preparation activity.
- Share mnemonic resources with students, such as Web sites and books, so they can continue to learn additional ways to strengthen their memory and study for exams. Placing these on your Web site may encourage parents to seek out these resources, as well.

BACK TO OUR TEAM ■

Remember that our co-teaching team in this chapter includes fifth-grade social studies teacher Mr. McClusky and special educator Miss Evans. They have been working together for a short time on the Iowa unit, and they are interested in mnemonics because their students are performing poorly on factually related quiz items. Miss Evans has been assuming the passive instructional role so far, and she is beginning to think that her role may not change unless she says something to Mr. McClusky. However, Miss Evans—like many teachers—is afraid to confront her senior colleague. However, she feels she has established herself and gained the trust and respect of Mr. McClusky, so she decides to share her need to contribute more to the co-taught class. Miss Evans could use the "sandwich technique" in this situation.

Sandwich Technique

After requesting time to visit with Mr. McClusky, briefly opening the conversation with some open-ended questions, then thanking him for meeting with her, Ms. Evans could say something like this:

Robert, I really enjoy co-teaching with you, and I have enjoyed brainstorming new ideas for our Iowa unit. However, so far, I have just been circulating around the room, ensuring students are following your directions. I am wondering if we can think of some ways I could be more involved in actually teaching the class.

Although there is no guarantee that Robert (Mr. McClusky) will be open to Miss Evan's request, at least Miss Evans has been authentic in her request and shared the concern from her perspective. The sandwich technique focuses on the issue and invites collaborative efforts to resolve the issue.

The Result

We will assume the best in this scenario—that Mr. McClusky really listened to his co-partner. As a result of their discussion, this team decided to use parallel teaching for the next few days. The class will be split in half, and each teacher will teach the same lessons to half the students. This model allows Miss Evans feel that she is making an impact on student learning, yet she does not need to instruct the entire class. In parallel teaching, both teachers operate from the same lesson plan to promote consistent learning among all students. Both teachers need to be confident in the subject matter, so the learning of students in their half is not jeopardized. In this situation, parallel teaching is an appropriate choice, because Miss Evans is a long-time resident of Iowa and is familiar with the content in the Iowa unit.

Therefore, the team does some coplanning for the next three days. They decide that each teacher will teach the FIRST-letter mnemonic strategy and share specific examples of each step related to the Iowa unit. On Day 2, they will teach the key word vocabulary method when they introduce new geography terms. Miss Evans will teach her class three vocabulary terms using this method, and Mr. McClusky will teach his students three different vocabulary words using this method. Then, on Day 3, students will come together and teach their partners their three vocabulary words, so the result will be that each student will learn six new vocabulary words. An outline of the teachers' basic lesson plans looks like this.

■ LESSON PLAN

Day 1

Advance organizer: Share objective, rationale, and connection such as: "Today we are going to learn a mnemonic strategy. This strategy will help you remember items for exams in all of your subjects. We have learned many important facts about our state, Iowa, and now we will learn a way to remember those facts."

K-W-L chart: Complete a "What I know, what I want to know, what I learned" (K-W-L) chart with the class to assess informally what they already know about mnemonics and what they want to know. Brainstorm different kinds and examples of mnemonics.

Instruction: Directly teach, using the overhead projector, the FIRST-letter mnemonic strategy. Describe each step and provide at least one example of each step using lists from the Iowa unit. Students take guided notes on this presentation.

Student practice: In groups of two or three, students practice each step of the FIRST-letter mnemonic strategy. Teachers provide a practice sheet (worksheet) containing various lists of social studies items to each group, and groups develop their own mnemonics for each list. Teachers circulate among their students and provide support as needed.

Sharing: Groups share some of the mnemonics they developed. Students place their completed practice sheets in their social studies folders.

Finish map work: If time remains, students work on their map activity (p. 139 of their text).

Closure: Before dismissal, return to the K-W-L chart and ask students what they learned about mnemonics and, in particular, the FIRST-letter mnemonic strategy. Provide specific feedback to students about their performance and dismiss students to their next class.

Preparation: Miss Evans agrees to develop and make copies of the practice worksheet, reserve an extra overhead projector, get some colored overhead markers, and make a classroom chart with the steps of the FIRST-letter mnemonic strategy. Mr. McClusky agrees to develop and make copies of the guided notes handout and to divide the class into the two main groups. Together, both teachers brainstorm examples they will each use in their teaching presentation.

Day 2

Advance organizer: Share objective, rationale, or connection, such as, "Today we will learn and practice a new vocabulary strategy. This method will help you remember vocabulary words and concepts from your classes. We have already learned modeling, definitions, and synonyms as vocabulary strategies."

Instruction: Using the overhead projector, directly teach the key word vocabulary method. Model the three steps of the strategy with social studies vocabulary words from a previous unit. Ask for student volunteers to draw the interactive image on the overhead for each example.

Student practice: In groups of two or three, students develop their own key words and interactive images using three new words chosen by the teacher from the Iowa unit. Teachers circulate among their students and offer assistance, as needed.

Sharing: Each group is asked to share their favorite key word example.

Finish map work and crossword puzzle: If time remains, students will continue to finish their map work and complete a crossword puzzle based on geography terms from the unit.

Closure: Before dismissal, ask the class the three steps of the key word strategy. Ask students to brainstorm other situations where they could use this strategy. Provide specific feedback to students about their performance and dismiss students to their next class.

Preparation: Miss Evans and Mr. McClusky agree on the three vocabulary words their class sections will use for student practice. They also agree on example words to use in their initial teaching presentations. Mr. McClusky already has copies of the crossword puzzle, which he will provide to Miss Evans.

Day 3

All students are brought together into the large group. A student from Miss Evans's group is paired with a student from Mr. McClusky's group, and each student teaches his partner his key word strategy for remembering his three vocabulary words. After partner teaching, the class reviews the FIRST-letter mnemonic strategy. With their partners, students look over their study guide for the upcoming quiz and develop ways to remember information and vocabulary words using the two strategies. Groups share their mnemonics with the class as a way to prepare for the upcoming quiz.

Preparation: As students enter the classroom, Mr. McClusky tells them whom they will be working with today. Miss Evans provides the advanced organizer and shares the plan and agenda. Both teachers circulate and provide feedback as students are peer-teaching. Both teachers call on students and teams to share their mnemonics as part of the class discussion. Mr. McClusky transitions the class to the study guide activity and provides directions for this part of the session. Both teachers circulate as students brainstorm ways to use strategies, and both teachers call on students to share their test preparation mnemonic strategies based on their study guide. Mr. McClusky provides closure for the lesson and reminds students of the upcoming quiz.

■ MNEMONICS AND OTHER CO-TEACHING MODELS

This chapter illustrated the parallel teaching model as a vehicle for teaching students mnemonic strategies. The remaining co-teaching models could also be used, as noted below:

- *One teach, one observe:* Mr. McClusky could teach the class the mnemonic strategy, while Miss Evans observes the class as well as Mr. McClusky's teaching behaviors. Perhaps Mr. McClusky wants to know if he is calling on boys and girls equally, students from various parts of the room equally, and students who raise their hands as well as those who do not raise their hands. Miss Evans could collect this data during his instruction.
- *One teach, one drift:* As students are taking guided notes over Mr. McClusky's presentation on mnemonics, Miss Evans could circulate, check student work, quietly remind students to remain on task, offer physical proximity as needed, and help students with their notes as needed.
- *Station teaching:* The teaching team could develop mnemonic learning stations that present different applications of the mnemonic strategies they have taught. In small groups, students rotate among all of the stations, thereby practicing many mnemonic strategies during a given class period. Each co-teacher could direct one station.
- *Alternate teaching:* Perhaps the co-teaching team observed that some students did not grasp the mnemonic strategy, or perhaps some students were absent during the initial mnemonic instruction. Mr. McClusky could pull those students aside to teach or reteach the strategies while Miss Evans leads the rest of the class.
- *Team teaching:* After agreeing on the lesson plan and their individual responsibilities for planning the lesson, both teachers could agree to present the lesson as a team. The co-teachers might agree to take the lead in certain parts of the lesson, but each teacher will feel free to add additional examples and explanations of the strategy steps.

SUMMARY   ■

This chapter focused on teaching mnemonics in co-taught inclusive classrooms. Mnemonics are an artificial memory aid imposed on the curriculum. Researchers have found mnemonics to be one of the most powerful techniques for teachers to present to students. This chapter presented examples of acronyms and visuals, the two main types of mnemonics. The chapter also reviewed an effective communication technique to use when confronting a co-teaching partner. The sandwich technique was illustrated within the scenario of one teacher being afraid to confront a more senior teacher. The chapter concluded by showing how mnemonics could be used in various lesson plans using various co-teaching models.

REFLECTIONS TO APPLICATION   ■

As co-teachers, have we . . .

- Discussed the importance of using mnemonics?
- Introduced several specific mnemonic strategies to our students?
- Infused mnemonics into our instructional routines?

ADDITIONAL RESOURCES   ■

Books

Mastropieri, M. A., & Scruggs, T. E. (1991). *Teaching students ways to remember: Strategies for learning mnemonically.* Cambridge, MA: Brookline Books.

Mastropieri, M. A., & Scruggs, T. E. (2006). Improving attention and memory. In M. A. Mastropieri & T. E. Scruggs (Eds.), *The inclusive classroom: Strategies for effective instruction* (3rd ed.; pp. 218–243). Columbus, OH: Prentice Hall/Merrill.

Schumaker, J. B., Bulgren, J. A., Deshler, D. D., & Lenz, B. K. (1998). *The recall enhancement routine.* Lawrence, KS: University of Kansas.

Articles

Bulgren, J. A., Schumaker, J. B., & Deshler, D. D. (1994). The effects of a recall enhancement routine on the test performance of secondary students with and without learning disabilities. *Learning Disabilities Research and Practice, 9,* 2–11.

Carney, R. N., & Levin, J. R. (2000). Mnemonic instruction with a focus on transfer. *Journal of Educational Psychology, 92,* 783–790.

Foil, C. R., & Alber, S. R. (2002). Fun and effective ways to build your students' vocabulary. *Intervention in School and Clinic, 37(3),* 131–140.

Fulk, B. J. M. (1994). Mnemonic keyword strategy training for students with learning disabilities. *Learning Disabilities Research and Practice, 9,* 179–185.

King-Sears, M. E., Mercer, C. D., & Sindelar, P. (1992). Toward independence with keyword mnemonics: A strategy for science vocabulary instruction. *Remedial and Special Education, 13,* 22–33.

Mastropieri, M. A., & Scruggs, T. E. (1998a). Constructing more meaningful relationships in the classroom: Mnemonic research into practice. *Learning Disabilities Research and Practice, 13,* 138–145.

Mastropieri, M. A., & Scruggs, T. E. (1998b). Enhancing school success with mnemonic strategies. *Intervention in School and Clinic, 33,* 201–208.

Mastropieri, M. A., Scruggs, T. E., Bakken, J. P., & Brigham, F. J. (1992). A complex mnemonic strategy for teaching states and capitals: Comparing forward and backward associations. *Learning Disabilities Research and Practice, 7,* 96–103.

Mastropieri, M. A., Scruggs, T. E., Fulk, B. J. M. (1990). Teaching abstract vocabulary with the keyword method: Effects on recall and comprehension. *Journal of Learning Disabilities, 23,* 92–96.

Mastropieri, M. A., Sweda, J., & Scruggs, T. E. (2000). Teacher use of mnemonic strategy instruction. *Learning Disabilities Research and Practice, 15,* 69–74.

Scruggs, T. E., & Mastropieri, M. A. (1992). Classroom applications of mnemonic instruction: Acquisition, maintenance and generalization. *Exceptional Children, 58,* 219–229.

Scruggs, T. E., & Mastropieri, M. A. (2000). Mnemonic strategies improve classroom learning and social behavior. *Beyond Behavior, 10*(1), 13–17.

Uberti, H. Z., Scruggs, T. E., & Mastropieri, M. A. (2003). Keywords make the difference! Mnemonic instruction in inclusive classrooms. *Teaching Exceptional Children, 10*(3), 56–61.

Web Sites

The Center for Research on Learning at the University of Kansas provides a quick one-page online reference that demonstrates word-based devices and combined mnemonic devices: http://itc.gsu.edu/academymodules/a304/support/xpages/a304b0_20600.html.

Members of the Division for Learning Disabilities (DLD) of the Council for Exceptional Children can access a free online tutorial on mnemonics: www.teachingld.org.

The National Center on Accessing Curriculum publishes two information briefs, *Teaching Sounds, Letters, and Letter-Sound Correspondences* and *These Methods Suggest a New Pedagogy for Literacy Development,* which demonstrate how mnemonics are used in the classroom: www.cast.org.

The Virginia Council for Learning Disabilities also provides information from Mastropieri and Scruggs: http://www.vcld.org/pages/newsletters/00_01_fall/mnemonic.htm.

5

Teaching So They Make Connections

Co-Teaching With Visuals

The 24 ninth graders in Mr. Edwin and Mr. Sanchez's ninth-grade Science 101: Fundamentals of Science class represent diverse learning styles, abilities, and cultures. This section is considered the "adjusted" science class, yet the course covers state standards. Years ago, due to their reading skill levels or other disabilities, some of these students would have received science instruction in the special education classroom. The special education teacher paralleled the general science curriculum as much as possible, but students were not exposed to a robust and challenging science curriculum, as he did not have adequate materials or a science background. Pull-out special education content courses at McKinley High School have been replaced with inclusion classes with push-in supports, such as co-teaching, because special education teachers are not highly qualified in those subjects. Further, McKinley administrators and faculty believe that students with mild disabilities profit by accessing the general curriculum.

Mr. Edwin and Mr. Sanchez have been co-teaching for two years. Mr. Edwin, a 10-year teacher, is highly qualified in science, and Mr. Sanchez, an 18-year teacher, has background as a speech-language pathologist and is one of the district's English as a second language (ESL) teachers; he co-teaches in several content classes. This team has adjusted well to co-teaching, and they have used most of the co-teaching models. Usually, Mr. Edwin presents the main information, and, as necessary, Mr. Sanchez rephrases and clarifies, presents information with students in their native language, makes necessary accommodations or modifications, and assists individuals or small groups. With this support, most students make satisfactory progress. The two teachers, however, have noticed that students answer some questions correctly but do not elaborate or expand on their responses. The team thinks they could enhance their instruction even more to help students

Authors' Note: We would like acknowledge Northern Illinois University students Amanda Theis and Elizabeth McDonald for their assistance in making the line drawings and visuals for this chapter.

make connections in the curriculum. Another issue with this team is parity. Mr. Sanchez has not said anything yet, but he has been feeling a bit more like a paraprofessional than an equal.

This team in a nutshell:

Grade level: 9

Classroom contextual factors: 24 students (12 have mild disabilities, reading challenges, or are ESL)

Subject: Science

Co-teaching stage: Expert

Interpersonal issue: Parity

Instructional challenge: Students are not making connections within the curriculum

---

■ VISUALS

Most of us have heard or said, "A picture is worth a thousand words." This expression also applies to many students in general education classrooms, whose learning would be enhanced if information was presented visually. For our discussion, *visuals* are defined as any instructional format or structure that provides students with a supplemental image that facilitates communication and understanding about a topic. Teachers may use a variety of names for these visuals, such as graphic organizers, semantic maps, webs, mind maps, and so forth.

This chapter emphasizes the importance of using visuals in co-taught classrooms. You will learn the importance of visuals, various kinds of visuals, and ways to use visuals. After reading this chapter, you will be able to do the following:

- Define and provide examples of visuals.
- Provide a rationale for using visuals in classrooms.
- Describe the use of several specific visuals.
- Describe the story telling communication method.

■ A RATIONALE FOR USING VISUALS

One reason to consider using visuals in your instruction is that they can be effective for many students. Some teachers might mistakenly think that visuals are *only* appropriate for students with poor auditory or language-processing skills, students with disabilities, or students whose native language is not English, yet we know that students who are gifted who often use visuals (rather than outlining or note taking) as a preferred study technique. According to Ellis and Howard (2007), visuals can be effective for *all* students. The complexity of the information, the amount of elaboration the learner uses when processing information, and students' memory and background knowledge all contribute to student success with visuals. These authors noted that visuals work best under the following conditions:

- The figure is developmentally appropriate for the students' background, knowledge, and experience with visuals.
- The level of assistance provided to students matches their developmental levels.
- The information on the visual matches students' background knowledge of the topic.
- The size and space of the visual is appropriate if students will be writing on the visual.
- The visual reflects students' independent reading and writing skills, so they can use it as a study and review tool.

Secondly, because visuals can be effective with all students, when used with all students, they often reduce the need for additional subsequent accommodations. Many teachers use visuals as part of universal designed instruction for learning (UDL), an approach that provides a number of ways to make learning accessible for students with disabilities. In other words, UDL encourages learning through a combination of flexible materials and methods that provide access, challenge, and engagement for each child. In their description of UDL, researchers at the Center for Applied Special Technology (CAST) note the importance of presenting content in multiple ways, providing multiple ways for students to express what they know, and having multiple options for student engagement. Incorporating charts, diagrams, or graphic representations of course material (with labels in descriptive text) is one way to use UDL. Many teachers have found that presenting information through more than one modality (such as leading a class discussion and, simultaneously, summarizing that information in a visual format) reaches more students than if the discussion occurred without any visual supports. As a matter of practice, when teachers present information in more than one modality and allow students to display what they have learned through more than one modality, fewer students require additional individualized accommodations.

Next, because so many different types and formats exist, visuals are very flexible and can be used in any subject or grade level. Teachers can use visuals before (for brainstorming and priming students' background knowledge), during (for taking notes), or after (for summarizing and retelling) instruction. Further, students can develop their own visuals. The instructional possibilities of using visuals are endless.

Finally, visuals have a solid research base. They have shown to be effective in improving reading comprehension, written comprehension, and content learning—including math. They have also been effective in helping students understand the relationship among and between ideas. Visuals have been found to support vocabulary, problem-solving skills, and writing fluency. In short, research documents a solid scientific basis for their use.

■ IS THE VISUAL REALLY A VISUAL?

Here is a question: When is a visual not a visual? Answer: When it is not visual. Imagine (and you probably have had this experience) attending a workshop where the presenter used dozens and dozens of PowerPoint slides. If all the slides contain narrative text (perhaps with bullets) but without accompanying icons, figures, pictures, clip art, animation, or illustrations, the presentation really is not visual, even if slides are in different background colors. Similarly, teachers may think they are using visuals, when their products (e.g., graphic organizers) actually contain only words. Our first tip for developing visuals, therefore, is this: make sure visuals accompany the text.

■ VARIOUS TYPES OF VISUALS

Most text can be supplemented with a visual or visuals to stimulate student interest and attention, support memory, and accommodate reading or processing issues. For example, teachers often make daily or weekly picture schedules for students with cognitive disabilities, autism, or traumatic brain injury. These schedules list the student's classes in sequential order with an accompanying icon for each class, such as a picture of a baseball for P.E. class or a picture of a sink and stove for cooking class. The student follows the schedule by noting the order of pictures if she is unable to read.

Similarly, many students benefit from a picture task analysis, which is a step-by-step illustration showing how to complete a task. The first step in writing a research paper, for example, might be to gather books, articles, and information from various Web sites on the chosen topic. Therefore, Step 1 of this picture task analysis might be "research topic from many different sources" with associated visual icons, such as a book, magazine, or computer. Clearly, the advantage of icons is that nonreaders understand the task. Picture task analysis is especially helpful for students with moderate or severe disabilities who can be successful when tasks are broken into sequential steps with adjoining pictures or illustrations.

Our remaining discussion focuses on just a few types of visuals, such as concept diagrams, concept maps, and other basic visual displays, often called maps or webs. These are more frequently used in general education classes with students with and without disabilities.

Concept diagrams are one way to teach a vocabulary word or concept thoroughly. Using this approach, the teacher chooses an important word or concept to be taught and completes the concept diagram sheet, which serves as the answer key. Although variations exist, the basic concept diagram sheet includes the definition of the word or concept; characteristics of the word or concept that are always, sometimes, and never present; and examples and nonexamples of the word or concept. The teacher presents the completed concept diagram to students via the board or overhead by revealing one part at a time (first the definition, then characteristics, then examples and nonexamples) and involves students by discussing each section before moving to the next. Students may copy the information on their own concept diagram, as appropriate. Because the concept diagram itself is not very visual, teachers may add pictures or icons to provide visual support. For example, students can label one quadrant "picture" and draw their own visual for the word or concept. Figure 5.1 shows an example of a completed concept diagram but one that could be improved with picture icons. Because this approach strategically introduces the complexities and subtleties of a word or concept, our experience has been that students thoroughly understand material presented in this format.

Figure 5.1   Completed Concept Diagram

Definition: A form of government in which citizens have the right to decide rules for that group.

Characteristics Present in the Concept

Always	Sometimes	Never
• Free and fair elections • Equal rights • Government based on majority rule	• Applies to groups and organizations • Involves several parties or platforms	• One person has absolute authority • Citizens not allowed to criticize their government

Examples | Nonexamples

All eleventh graders elect their class officials.

One teacher in a school develops the dress code for all teachers.

All district teachers vote on their contract.

Some people get to cast two votes and others get zero votes.

All U.S. citizens vote for their president.

The king appoints his successor to the throne.

Concept maps, sometimes called graphic organizers or visual-spatial displays (Carnine, Silbert, Kame'euni, & Tarver, 2004), are another way to present material visually. They are often used to support content area reading, because they help students understand the chapter's content and structure. A concept map visually represents a body of knowledge, including the critical concepts, vocabulary, ideas, events, generalizations, and facts, usually in a diagram or other visual display. Students viewing the concept map gain a holistic view of the body of knowledge before reading the material. Carnine et al. note six variations of concept maps:

1. The hierarchy map depicts a hierarchical body of knowledge, such as the organization of the federal government.

2. The diagram shows the relationship of parts to the whole, such as the four layers of the atmosphere.

3. Compare-and-contrast, in chart form, illustrates how two or more items are similar and different, such as different climates, common plants, and animals in various biomes.

4. The time line depicts important events in sequential order, such as events surrounding the Stamp Act.

5. Process shows a process or cycles, such as how cotton cloth is manufactured or the rock cycle.

6. Multiple structures notes the relationship and includes examples of several related concepts, such as organisms, kingdoms, and species.

Figures 5.2 and 5.3 provide examples of two of these types of concept maps.

A suggested teaching sequence (Carnine et al., 2004) when using any of these six maps includes the following five steps:

1. Determine the critical content you want to preteach students.

2. Organize concepts in the appropriate visual structure.

3. Design the completed concept map.

4. Create a partially competed map that is distributed to students for completion during instruction.

5. Create a blank concept map that can be used later as a review activity to re-create items from memory.

During initial instruction, teachers introduce information on the concept map, proceeding logically and stressing the relationships among vocabulary concepts, events, details, and facts. These concept maps serve as a way to preteach information to students before they independently

Figure 5.2   Concept Map: Diagram

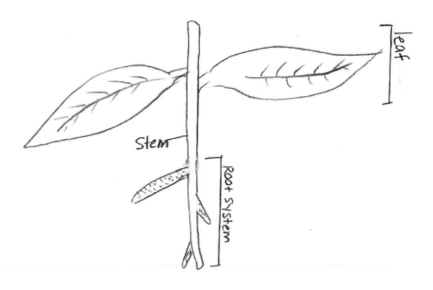

Figure 5.3   Concept Map: Compare/Contrast

	Climate	Common Plants	Tourist Spots
Arizona	Hot and dry summers Mild winters	Cactus Cotton	Grand Canyon O.K. Corral Scottsdale Historical Museum
Wisconsin	Wet spring and summers Cold snowy winter	Corn Cranberries	Milwaukee Art Museum Wisconsin Dells Door County

read expository material. These visuals also provide a powerful way for students with reading challenges to access the general curriculum.

The final structure we discuss is often referred to as a map or web. Often, these structures contain circles or other geometric figures (squares, rectangles, triangles, etc.) representing concepts and lines connecting those concepts that illustrate a relationship. Figures 5.4 through 5.6 show an example of a web used on the first day of an algebra class to introduce students to the course. First, we show the web containing only narrative text (Figure 5.4), and then we show the same web with connectors (words or short phrases that connect the main idea, algebra, with subpoints) in Figure 5.5. Notice that the connectors make a complete phrase or sentence when read, starting with the word *Algebra*. For example, students read *Algebra teaches Order of Operations, Algebra introduces Various Symbols,* and so forth. Students can also provide their own connectors. Connectors are helpful, because they make the relationships among and between topics and subtopics explicit. Without them, students may forget or misunderstand connections. Finally, Figure 5.6 includes the web with connectors and some visuals. Symbols enhance the web even further. We have noticed that some students remember the symbols on the graphic before they remember the words. In other words, symbols act as memory trigger for some students more so than text.

Figure 5.4   Web With Text Only

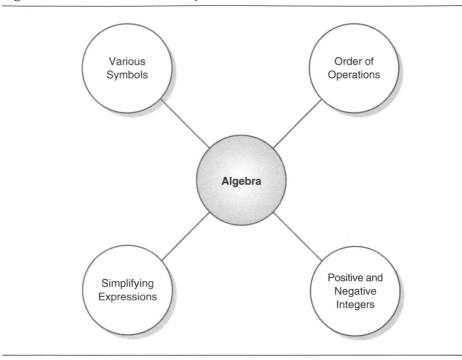

Figure 5.5   Web With Connectors

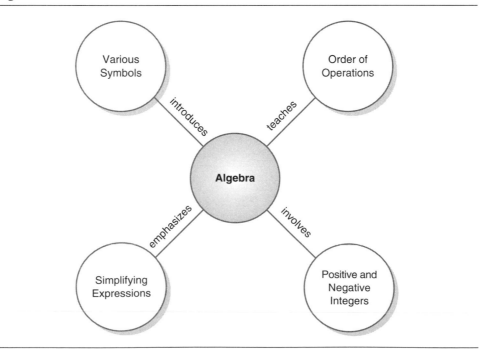

Figure 5.6   Web With Connectors and Visuals

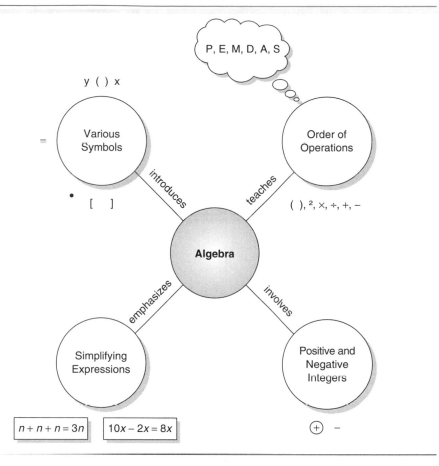

TEACHER BEHAVIORS ■

Regardless of which type of visual used with your students, we offer the following guidelines to inform your practice.

- Use visuals liberally in your instruction. Imagine being a student going from class to class and listening to teachers talk. Auditory information can overload some students, taxing their energy and attention. Pairing auditory input with visuals supports student learning by offering a second processing modality that some students prefer. Our experience has been that when students are presented information in more than one modality, they often attend more readily and retain more information.
- Make the visual truly visual. Webs containing only words (such as Figures 5.4 and 5.5) are not visual. Adding clip art or other basic structures adds the visual dimension. Another option is to have students add their own visuals to the basic web, thus adding personal meaning.
- Use connectors. These words or phrases help students remember how topics are connected. Make sure they sound like a complete sentence when read, but keep the connectors short and to the point. You can use the same connector more than once on a web.

- Chose the visual that matches your lesson objective. For example, circles with arrows often are used to represent a cycle, feedback loop, or cause and effect; various geometric shapes are often used to show different steps in a flowchart; and a Venn diagram is frequently used to show comparison and contrast. Some sample graphic organizer patterns are shown in Figure 5.7.

Figure 5.7   Sample Structures

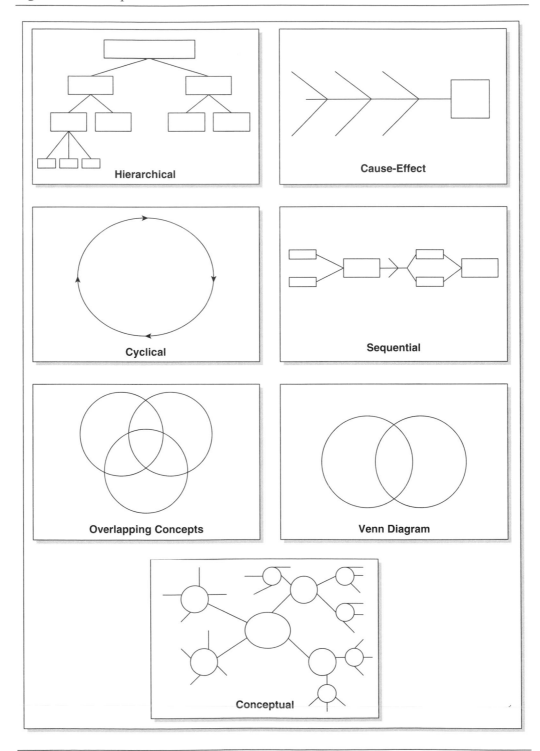

- Teach visuals explicitly by telling and showing students how the visual is used. In co-taught classrooms like Mr. Edwin and Mr. Sanchez's, as one teacher leads the class by explaining content from the chapter or reading material, the partner can develop and show the visual and reinforce content by explaining how the visual summarizes the discussion. Teachers can also demonstrate how to use the completed visual as a review tool by using a self-checking procedure. Students cover up parts of the visual and test themselves on remembering hidden parts.
- Consider the five-step instructional sequence mentioned earlier.
- Teach students how to make their own visuals. After having experience with various visuals, students may be ready to construct their own, perhaps first with a partner or with teacher guidance. Some student-generated visuals are as good—or better—than those in textbooks.

BACK TO OUR TEAM   ■

The co-teaching team in this chapter includes a general education, highly qualified science teacher and an ESL teacher. They have been working together for a while and have found a comfortable teaching arrangement. A few recent issues, however, have signaled lack of parity for Mr. Sanchez. He has noticed that Mr. Edwin is making instructional decisions and homework policies without consulting him. Also, he overheard some students talking in the hall about both teachers in a manner that caused him to question how students perceive his role.

Storytelling Technique

After thinking about what he should do, Mr. Sanchez decided to talk to Mr. Edwin about what he heard in the hall. Overhearing students from their science class provided Mr. Sanchez with the perfect opportunity to bring up his concern. He decided to use a storytelling communication format to share his concern by saying: "Eddie, yesterday in the hall, I overheard two students from our science class talking. They did not know I could hear them. As they were talking, they mentioned their science teacher is Mr. Edwin who has a helper named Perez—the guy who works with students who need help with English. I am now wondering if students see me as the assistant who just helps students with English. I was also surprised they did not even know my last name." Mr. Sanchez then gently reminded Mr. Edwin that he could not recall the last time he was referred to by his last name in class.

The Result

Somewhat surprised, Mr. Edwin indicated that his informality when using the name *Perez* in front of the students was not an intentional way of showing disrespect and from now on, he would make sure Mr. Sanchez was treated and perceived as an equal. The two brainstorm ways to ensure greater parity—including referring to both teachers as "Mr."; having both names on the door, the board, and in parent communications; allowing both teachers to teach all students; and revisiting ways to ensure that neither teacher is surprised by new instructional approaches or homework or behavior policies.

The two teachers also use this opportunity to discuss student concerns—especially their observation that students can locate factual information from their text and other reading material, they can answer factual questions on their study guides and quizzes, but they are having difficulty making connections within the discipline. Wondering if their instructional and assessment practices might be partly responsible, the team decides to ask additional, higher-level questions; add higher-level reflection questions on lab activities; and include at least one short-answer or essay question on science assessments. The two also wonder if using various forms of graphic organizers or visuals might help students make curricular connections.

Because much of science is interrelated, visuals can be used to present many concepts and processes. Rather than moving to the next topic, the team decides to spend the next week reviewing previously learned material with the purpose of using visuals to model connections with known content. The team plans for the following week.

■ LESSON PLAN

Day 1

First, Mr. Edwin calls students' attention to the teacher names on the board, clarifies the roles of both teachers, and reaffirms their equal roles. He emphasizes that both teachers are responsible for all students and that this week, the two teachers will be using some different approaches.

Advance organizer: Mr. Sanchez shows various examples of visuals and graphic organizers from the text and Internet and some that he has created. He asks the class what these have in common and if they use visuals much in other classes, and he emphasizes the importance of using visuals in science. He notes that this week the class will be doing several activities using different kinds of graphic organizers. He concludes, "This week, we will be learning various structures, graphic organizers, or visuals. These will help you remember and organize information from science and help you make connections among and between topics. We have used charts and tables in science, and now we will learn other ways to organize information."

Introduce topic: The team shares the topic for today, which is environmental issues. Both teachers lead the class in a think-pair-share activity, where student partners brainstorm three of the most pressing environmental issues facing the world today. Mr. Ellis asks for ideas, while Mr. Sanchez writes student-generated topics on the board. The class shares several issues. Mr. Ellis then asks the class to vote on the top three of all ideas listed. After some class discussion, the class votes on their top three.

Structured written activity: Mr. Sanchez distributes a matrix chart with a place for students to list the three environmental issues on the top of the chart with rows on the left for indicating causes, effects, and possible solutions. He also provides each student with a blank piece of white paper. As a class, the students discuss each issue and complete their charts while Mr. Sanchez models this on the overhead.

Introduce conceptual visual: Mr. Ellis indicates that another way to organize information is with a visual. With Mr. Sanchez remaining at the overhead, Mr. Ellis directs students to use their white paper to make their visual. Using information from their chart, Mr. Ellis asks students questions such as these: What is the main topic we discussed today? What were the three environmental issues we thought were most important? What were some causes of the first issue? As students use their charts to answer, Mr. Sanchez develops a conceptual web on the overhead. Students copy this web on their white paper. Mr. Sanchez includes connectors such as "is caused by" or "leads to" or "may be solved through" and stops periodically to read the web. Mr. Sanchez also uses different colored overhead pens for causes, effects, and solutions and a different color for the connectors. Many students do the same.

Discussion: Both teachers engage the class in a discussion of two ways of displaying science knowledge—the matrix or chart and the conceptual web.

Homework: The class is not used to having homework, so the last few minutes of class could be used to do this activity, or students could do this as homework. Mr. Sanchez notes that the conceptual web is helpful in its present form but an improvement would be to add visuals or icons. He provides an example. He emphasizes that each person learns differently, and some students may remember more when visuals are included. Therefore, the homework assignment is to draw in visuals for at least five web items.

Closure: Before students are dismissed, both teachers ask factual and higher-level questions based on the discussion and the completed chart and matrix and web. Teachers provide feedback to students regarding their behavior and work, remind them of the homework, and dismiss them to their next class.

Day 2

Introduction or sharing: As students enter, they pick up pieces of white paper. The class begins by both teachers asking for volunteers to share their competed web. Several students volunteer. Students submit their webs to the teachers.

Advanced organizer: Mr. Ellis reviews that the conceptual map or web is effective to use when the main topic (environmental issues) has several subtopics (e.g., global warming, endangered species, and unsafe water) and those subtopics have several subpoints (e.g., causes, effects, and possible solutions). All of those points and subpoints remind us of a web—like a spider's web that goes off in different directions. He notes, "Today we will learn a different way to present science information when we need to compare and contrast. This will help you see quickly what structures have in common and what is different about them."

Introduce topic: Mr. Ellis begins by asking students to think about what they recall about plant cells and animal cells, which the class recently studied. He provides five minutes for students (in pairs or trios) to review their notes, text, portfolios, or completed science labs to answer the question: How are plant and animal cells alike and different? After five minutes, he asks teams to share, and as students respond, Mr. Sanchez writes their responses on the board under the columns "plant cells" and "animal cells."

Introduce Venn diagram: Mr. Ellis indicates that another way to organize information is with a Venn diagram. With Mr. Sanchez at the overhead, Mr. Ellis directs students to use their white paper to make the Venn diagram, like the one Mr. Sanchez is modeling. Mr. Ellis asks students to use the information from their charts to answer questions such as these: What characteristics are *only* found in plant cells? What characteristics are *only* found in animal cells? What characteristics are common to *both*? As students respond, Mr. Sanchez and the students add that characteristic to the appropriate place on their Venn diagrams. Periodically, Mr. Sanchez verbally summarizes what has been written and points to corresponding diagram parts.

Discussion: Both teachers engage the class in a discussion on the use of a Venn diagram. The class brainstorms other science topics that could be represented through a Venn diagram, as well as topics and uses in other classes.

Homework: Mr. Sanchez notes that the Venn diagram summarizes a lot of information in its present form but an improvement would be to add visuals or icons. He provides an example. Similar to yesterday, the homework assignment, which could also be completed during the last few minutes of class, is to draw in visuals for at least three of the items on the Venn diagram *and* to write a five-sentence summary of the information from the chart. Students may use their texts, the Internet, or other materials as needed. Students may use class computers to view Web sites with illustrated plant and animal cells. Mr. Sanchez distributes a template for students to use for their summary:

Animal and plant cells are alike and different in several ways. Both animal and plant cells have_____. Only animal cells have _____. Only plant cells have _____. These are the main similarities and differences scientists have found in animal and plant cells.

Students use their Venn diagrams and any other resources to complete the assignment.

Closure: Before students are dismissed, both teachers ask questions based on the discussion and the completed Venn diagram. Teachers provide feedback to students regarding their behavior and work, remind them of the homework, and dismiss them to their next class.

Day 3

Introduction or sharing: As students enter, they pick up pieces of white paper. The class begins by both teachers asking for volunteers to share their illustrated Venn diagram and summary. Several students volunteer. Students submit their homework assignments.

Advanced organizer: Mr. Sanchez reviews uses of the web and Venn diagram. He notes, "Today we will learn a way to present science information when a process is involved. This will help you quickly see the process as a whole as well as the steps in the process."

Introduce topic: Mr. Sanchez says, "In health class, you have recently studied the digestive system. This is an example of a process, or a series of steps. Today, we will use a different type of visual to represent that process." Mr. Sanchez asks students to think about which body parts are involved in the digestive process. The class brainstorms various body parts, and Mr. Ellis writes these on the board. Next, the class orders their list, beginning with the body part where digestion begins. Mr. Ellis asks, "How can we be sure our order is correct?" Several students suggest checking their health text, science text, and the Internet. While volunteers check those sources, Mr. Ellis introduces the cycle diagram.

Introduce cycle diagram: With Mr. Ellis at the overhead, Mr. Sanchez directs students to use their white paper to make the cycle diagram, like the one Mr. Ellis is making. Mr. Sanchez asks students to use the information from their list, which was verified by students doing additional research, to answer questions such as these: What is the first step in the digestive process? How can we summarize that? What is the second step? How can we summarize that step? As students respond, Mr. Ellis and the students write short phrases describing each step of the cycle on their paper. They add arrows to indicate sequence and connectors to support transitions. Periodically, both teachers ask students to summarize verbally.

Discussion: Both teachers engage the class in a discussion on the use of the cycle diagram. The class brainstorms other processes represented through this format.

Homework: By now, students know they need to add visuals to the cycle diagram, so they begin. Some students draw in various body parts, while others use the computer to print off clip art or other images. In addition to adding pictures, students respond in writing to two higher-level questions regarding the digestive system.

Closure: Before students are dismissed, both teachers ask questions based on the discussion and the completed diagram. Teachers provide feedback to students regarding their behavior and work, remind them of the homework, and dismiss them to their next class.

Day 4

Introduction or sharing: As students enter, they pick up a white piece of paper and a one-page written summary (written at students' reading level) of information regarding the food pyramid, serving sizes, wise food choices, and so forth. The summary does *not* include any visuals or pictures of the food pyramid. The class begins by both teachers asking for volunteers to share their completed cycle diagrams. Several students volunteer. Students submit their homework. Both teachers review all previously learned visual structures.

Advanced organizer: To add variety, both teachers decide to do a short role-play, with one of them pretending to be hungry, wanting a snack, and thinking about getting a candy bar and a soda from the vending machine. The partner stops the role-play action and asks the class if this is a wise choice for a snack. Students respond. The teachers offer a guiding question such as "What can guide our eating decisions so that we get the appropriate amounts of nutrients in our diet?" The students recall the food pyramid from their health class.

Introduce topic: The teachers note that the food pyramid will be the basis of their discussion today. To review that information, the class orally reads the food pyramid handout. Mr. Ellis then asks questions from the handout such as these: Which types of food should we eat the most of? The least of? Mr. Sanchez writes brief notes on the board based on student responses. Then, Mr. Ellis notes that the food pyramid is an example of a hierarchical structure, where we have a lot of something at one level and gradually less and less at other levels. "Today," he says, "we will use a different type of visual to represent the food pyramid."

Introduce hierarchical visual: With Mr. Sanchez at the overhead, Mr. Ellis directs students to use their white paper to make the hierarchical diagram like the one Mr. Sanchez is making. Using notes on the board, Mr. Ellis asks students questions such as these: What food group belongs in this level [pointing to the largest level]? How do you know? What food group belongs in the next level? How do you know? As students respond, Mr. Sanchez and the students complete their visuals. Periodically, both teachers ask students to summarize verbally.

Discussion: Both teachers engage the class in a discussion on the use of the hierarchical diagram. The class brainstorms other processes that could be represented through this format.

Homework: The homework assignment is to add visuals to their structure and answer three "what if" questions regarding unbalanced diets—for example, What would happen if someone did not have a sufficient amount of dairy products in his diet?

Closure: In addition to providing feedback to students and dismissing them to their next class, the two teachers provide one more role-play, but this time the hungry teacher chooses a healthy snack instead of a candy bar or chips and pop.

Day 5

Introduction or sharing: The class begins by sharing their homework.

Advanced organizer: After reviewing the visual structures (conceptual, Venn diagram, cyclical, and hierarchical), Mr. Edwin and Mr. Sanchez group students and provide each small group with copies of a one-page text at the appropriate reading level on a particular science topic. One group may have a reading selection on fundamental information on genetics, while another group may have information about recycling. Each group's task is to develop a visual that summarizes the information from their handout. The previously developed visuals are displayed as references, and both teachers circulate among all groups to offer assistance. Groups develop their visual (with pictures and connectors) and, time permitting, present them to the class.

■ VISUALS AND OTHER CO-TEACHING MODELS

This chapter illustrated team teaching, with two teachers sharing equal responsibilities in the lessons. During certain points in the lessons, each teacher had a certain role (e.g., drawing the visual or leading the class in discussion), but at other times, roles were blended. Other co-teaching models could also be used, as described below:

- *One teach, one observe:* Because these teachers set a goal to increase the percentage of higher-level questions asked in class, as one teacher leads the class in discussions and orally reviews, the partner could record data on the type of questions asked as well as the amount of student accuracy on various types of questions.

- *One teach, one drift:* Although Mr. Ellis is the content expert, Mr. Sanchez can also lead instruction, allowing Mr. Ellis to drift, support students, and view instruction from a different perspective. For example, perhaps as Mr. Sanchez demonstrates how to complete visuals, Mr. Ellis could drift to observe how much time students take to fill in their visuals and which students copy readily from the board and which students make copying errors. He could also provide immediate feedback to students regarding their visuals.
- *Parallel teaching:* Mr. Ellis and Mr. Sanchez might want to use parallel teaching to reinforce the concept of parity between both teachers. Any of the lessons noted above could be modified to include each teacher teaching the lesson to half the class.
- *Station teaching:* Rather than the application activity the teachers planned for Day 5, they could have used station teaching. Each station could contain a short science passage with the task of developing a visual based on that selection. Each station could also request a different type of visual. To save some time, perhaps each station could contain a partially developed visual based on the selection, and students would complete the visual.
- *Alternate teaching:* If either teaching partner observed students struggling with translating text into a visual or they were aware of students who needed an additional challenge, those identified students could be pulled to the side to do some review or enrichment activities on visuals with one of the co-teachers.

SUMMARY ■

This chapter introduced the use of several types of visuals in co-taught classrooms. Visuals have various names, such as semantic maps, mind maps, and graphic organizers. The beauty of these structures is they can be used at any grade level and in any subject and they benefit all students—not just those with language or learning issues. Despite visuals' wide applicability and strong research base, teachers often rely on class discussions and lectures to convey content area information, thereby reducing the effectiveness of their instruction. Co-taught classrooms are ideal for frequently using visuals, as one teacher can lead class discussion and brainstorming while the other develops and displays the visual. This chapter emphasized using connectors, infusing icons or pictures, and teaching students how to develop their own visuals. The storytelling technique was presented as an effective communication method when one co-teacher has heard comments from others that need to be shared.

REFLECTIONS TO APPLICATION ■

As co-teachers, have we . . .

- Discussed the importance of using visuals?
- Introduced several different types of visuals to our students?
- Infused visuals into our instructional routines?

◼ ADDITIONAL RESOURCES

Books

Bellanca, J. (2007). *A guide to graphic organizers: Helping students organize and process content for deeper meaning* (2nd ed.). Thousand Oaks, CA: Corwin Press.

Bromley, K., Irwin-Devitis, L., & Hires, D. (1999). *Graphic organizers (grades K–8).* New York: Scholastic.

Ellis, E. (2004). *Makes sense literacy think-sheets.* Lillian, AL: GraphicOrganizers.com

Hyerle, D. (2004). *Student successes with thinking maps: School-based research, results, and models for achievement using visual tools.* Thousand Oaks, CA: Corwin Press.

Rose, D. H., & Meyer, A. (2006). *A practical reader in Universal Design for Learning.* Cambridge, MA: Harvard Education Press.

Articles

Capretz, K., Ricker, B., & Sasak, A. (2003). *Improving organizational skills through the use of graphic organizers.* Master's research project, Saint Xavier University and Skylight Professional Development, Chicago & Glenview, IL. (ERIC Document Reproduction Service No. ED473056)

DiCecco, V. M., & Gleason, M. M. (2002). Using graphic organizers to attain relational knowledge from expository text. *Journal of Learning Disabilities, 34,* 306–321.

Fisher, A. L. (2001). Implementing graphic organizer notebooks: The art and science of teaching content. *Reading Teacher, 55*(2), 116–120.

Software and Web Sites

CAST: Transforming education through Universal Design for Learning. Retrieved March 1, 2008, from http://www.cast.org

Inspiration is a software program that uses integrated diagram and outline views to help students in Grades 6–12 create graphic organizers and expand topics into writing. See http://www.inspiration.com for more information.

Kidspiration is a software program for students in Grades K–5 to help them develop thinking, literacy, and number skills. Students use graphic organizers to explore ideas and relationships across curricular areas. See http://www.inspiration.com for more information.

Makes Sense Strategies is a software collection of graphic organizers for K–12 instruction in vocabulary, reading, writing, and content area learning. The software also includes PowerPoint presentations that address various applications of graphic organizers. See http://www.graphicorganizers.com or http://www.lanettcityschools.org/makesense/start%20MakesSense.pdf for more information.

Thinking Maps Inc., an educational consulting and publishing company specializing in providing professional staff development for K–12 schools, develops software programs and other materials. The company's focus is to implement Thinking Maps®, a common visual language for learning within and across disciplines. See http://www.thinkingmaps.com for links to its products.

6

Teaching So They Become More Independent

Co-Teaching Using Study Skills and Learning Strategies

Fourth-grade co-teachers Ms. Davis (special educator) and Mr. Patel (general educator) have been co-teaching for four weeks. Ms. Davis is known as the bubbly, enthusiastic, nurturing, always cheery teacher who frequently volunteers, sees the positive in every situation, and notes potential in every child. Sometimes her enthusiasm is a bit "much" for others, but this really is her personality. Therefore, when the opportunity came to co-teach, she willingly accepted the challenge. Ms. Davis has been teaching special education at the elementary level for 12 years—all at Madison Elementary School, which is located in a lower socioeconomic and quite diverse part of town. She views teaching children with disabilities as her passion and life work and has done much in her school to support children and families, such as leading fund-raising activities and food and clothing drives.

Mr. Patel is a second-year general education teacher who enjoys working with this age group because he feels he can have discussions with children at this age and teach them to become independent and responsible. He has high expectations for students and feels that part of his responsibility is to prepare students for their middle school transition. He identifies with many of these children as he grew up in this neighborhood, and he knows, from experience, that hard work and persistence pay off.

Due to a large number of fourth graders in Madison Elementary School with Individualized Education Plans in language arts skills (especially written language), *poor student scores in writing for students with and without disabilities, and the inclusion philosophy at Madison, Principal Edwards encourages innovative instructional approaches, such as co-teaching. Staff development presentations during the last two years have focused on inclusion, differentiating instruction, and scientifically based research methods.*

This co-teaching team has been working together for four weeks. Generally, they have used the one-teach, one-assist model, with Ms. Davis assisting students and alternative teaching. Ms. Davis works with different groups of students for preteaching, reteaching, and catching students up after extended absences. Ms. Davis has also been leading daily oral language (DOL) activities.

The issue is that even in this third quarter, although the content of their papers is satisfactory, students are still making numerous mechanical errors. They catch errors on DOL activities, but those editing skills are not transferring to their written work. Mr. Patel is getting visibly upset about this, and students are receiving low writing scores. This is quite upsetting to the students as well as Ms. Davis.

This team in a nutshell:

Grade level: 4

Classroom contextual factors: 26 students; 7 students with learning disabilities

Subject: Language arts (writing)

Co-teaching stage: Beginning

Interpersonal issue: Dealing with frustration in professional manner

Instructional challenge: Students have not mastered or generalized proofreading or editing skills and strategies

---

■ STUDY SKILLS AND LEARNING STRATEGIES

"Give a man a fish, and he eats for a day. Teach a man to fish, and he eats for a lifetime." This Chinese proverb captures the philosophy of teaching students study skills and learning strategies. Study skills and learning strategies are techniques that help students work more efficiently and independently.

This chapter focuses on using study skills and learning strategies in co-taught classrooms. You will learn various study skills and learning strategies to use at various grade levels, with an emphasis on strategies for editing written language. After reading this chapter, you will be able to do the following:

- Provide examples of various study skills and learning strategies.
- Articulate a rationale for incorporating study skills and learning strategies into the curriculum.

- Explain ways to incorporate study skills and learning strategies in co-taught classrooms.
- Describe the word picture communication skill.

WHAT ARE STUDY SKILLS AND LEARNING STRATEGIES?

Study skills are skills that students use to acquire, record, remember, and use information for learning. Using this definition, various study skills come to mind:

Acquire information: Students read, listen, watch, think, and do.

Record information: Students underline, take notes, outline, use an assignment book, or use audiotape or videotape.

Remember information: Students use mnemonics, chunk or group items, quiz themselves, and use verbal rehearsal strategies.

Use information: Students use reference materials, apply study skills to various situations, apply test taking skills, use time management skills, and use graphic aids.

These are just a few of the study skills that can be incorporated into any classroom at any grade. Even kindergarten students can learn the importance of critical study skills such as keeping their area organized, listening to others, and following directions.

LEARNING STRATEGIES

Some authors (e.g., Sabornie & deBettencourt, 2004) differentiate study skills from learning strategies. Although these overlap, learning strategies tend to be more specific and include specific steps for students to follow. Learning strategies also often involve metacognitive skills organized around a mnemonic, so students can remember the steps in a task (such as FOIL, which stands for multiply first terms, then outermost terms, then innermost terms, and finally last terms when multiplying binomials). For our discussion, we are not going to differentiate between study skills and learning strategies, because the end purpose for both is to help students become more successful, efficient, and independent learners.

A RATIONALE FOR TEACHING STUDY SKILLS AND LEARNING STRATEGIES

We offer several reasons for incorporating study skills into the curriculum. First, many students with and without disabilities do not have good study skills. Even students who have good study skills often do not generalize those skills to different settings or situations. For example, students may have been taught how to use semantic mapping as a reading comprehension tool, but they may not see its value as a prewriting tool unless they are specifically taught this "new" application. Also, being able to apply study skills is especially important with the increase in testing and accountability in today's schools.

Next, successful students use good study skills. Our experience has been that success in school depends largely on one's study skills. We know students with cognitive disabilities who have made the general education honor roll while students who were gifted in the same classes had report cards with Cs. Clearly, success in school today stems, in part, from good study skills.

Next, teaching study skills helps students later in their adult lives. Study skills are important not only for school work completion and success but also for completing tasks outside of school. For example, learning how to vary one's reading rate depending on the reading purpose is critical for reading the newspaper, scanning the phone book, or reviewing legal documents. Similarly, learning how to use reference materials is an important skill related to using the phone book and ordering materials from catalogues.

Finally, teachers can (and we believe should) teach study skills. Although some students will develop good study skills without teacher instruction, many students need specific instruction to become efficient learners. Students with disabilities often need more explicit instruction in using a study skill or learning strategy than others. Infusing study skills and learning strategies into the curriculum can help all students become more efficient learners.

■ EXAMPLES OF VARIOUS STUDY SKILLS AND LEARNING STRATEGIES

Here are just a few examples of study skills and learning strategies that can be taught at various levels. They are arranged by subject.

Lower Elementary

General Study Skills

- Listening skills can be introduced by playing various listening games in class and discussing how students performed. Also, one can do a particular action that has a sound, such as bouncing a ball in class when no one expects it, and then ask students how many times the ball was bounced. Periodically doing these activities (especially when students do not expect them) reminds students of the importance of good listening skills.
- Note-taking skills can be introduced by sharing a short "lecture" with students on an interesting topic; reading a short, interesting book; or showing a short video clip and having students write important information as they watch and listen. Discuss as a group and show a model of good notes.

Math Calculation

- The DRAW strategy (Morin & Miller, 1998) includes these steps:
  - Discover the sign (+, −, ×, ÷).
  - Read the problem ($7 \times 3 = ?$).
  - Answer or draw and check (answer if you are sure or draw a picture to show the answer, such as three groups of seven pencils).
  - Write the answer.

- Several math fact strategies and rules can be incorporated into the math curriculum, such as the following:
  - Anything $\times 0 = 0$.
  - Anything $+ 0 =$ itself.
  - The 9s pattern, such as $9 \times 5 = 45$, where the digits in the product (45) always add up to 9 and the first digit in the product (4) is 1 less than the multiplier (5).
  - The plus-1 strategy for early addition, where when you add 1, you say the next number.
  - The commutative relationship between facts: $3 + 6 = 9$, so $6 + 3 = 9$.
  - Fact families, doubles, and count-bys (count by 2, 3, etc.).

Math Story Problems

- Early instruction teaches students how to translate four key phrases—*get more, get rid of, end with, and how many*—into symbols. *Get more* translates into a plus sign, *get rid of* to a minus sign, *end with* to an equal sign, and *how many* to an empty box. (Stein, Kinder, Silbert, & Carnine, 2006).

Reading Comprehension

- An early comprehension strategy involving passages that involve one person doing a series of actions can be taught with this rule: name the person and tell the main thing the person did in all the sentences. When distracter sentences appear in the passage, the rule for creating a list of main ideas changes to this: tell the main thing the person or group did in most of the sentences (Carnine, Silbert, Kame'enui, & Tarver, 2004). For example, teachers could introduce the following passage by indicating that *most* of the sentences tell what a person did (Carnine et al.).

  Myrna Mae went to the pool and changed into her swimsuit. She swam six lengths of the pool. She likes swimming. She practiced the backstroke. She talked to her friends. She later went out to lunch with Arlo.

Reading Decoding

- The strategy for learning regular words (any word in which each letter makes its common sound), such as VC (vowel-consonant), CVC, VCC, CVCC, CCVC, and CCVCC, is to sound out the word and then translate the blended sounds into the complete word.
- Approaches for learning irregular words, or sight words (words where letters do not make their common sound), involve memorizing the word and using context clues.

Written Language

- A strategy for basic sentences is that sentences are a complete thought with a subject and a verb.
- As children write stories, they are taught elements of narratives, such as title, characters, and setting, and—eventually—goal; problem, or conflict and action; climax; and resolution. The strategy is that their story must include all these elements.

Upper Elementary

General Study Skills

- As students receive more homework, demonstrate how to complete their daily planner or assignment notebook. Also, show how to break an assignment (such as a book report) into several, doable sequential parts.
- Students can assess how they use their time by keeping a weekly calendar, with hour increments, where they indicate how they spent each hour. They calculate the number of hours doing various activities during the week and assess if they are using time well.
- When students begin using textbooks, review the parts of the textbook, the importance of key features such as bold and italicized print, captions, summaries, and other features.

Math

- Story problem strategies often include the following steps:
  - Read the problem out loud.
  - Look for important words and circle them.
  - Draw pictures to tell what is happening.
  - Write down the math sentence.
  - Write the answer.

- Students can be taught to eliminate irrelevant details in word problems by underlining the question and circling given parts of the problem.

Reading Comprehension

- If students already can identify main ideas and details, they can use the RAP strategy (Schumaker, Denton, & Deshler, 1984). The steps are as follows:
  - **R**ead the paragraph.
  - **A**sk yourself the main idea and two details from the paragraph.
  - **P**ut the main idea and details into your own words.

- Teach students strategies for three different types of comprehension questions:
  - *Literal:* The answer is directly from the passage, so go to the passage for the answer.
  - *Search and think:* Be cautious and use different parts of the passage to answer a question.
  - *On my own:* Stop and think carefully and use proof from the passage.

- Six effective comprehension strategies include the following (Carnine et al., 2004):
  - Monitoring comprehension
  - Using graphic and semantic organizers
  - Answering questions
  - Generating questions
  - Recognizing story structure
  - Summarizing

Reading Decoding

- Students can learn the six syllable types and the common strategy for each one:
  - *Closed:* A closed syllable has one vowel, ends in at least one consonant, and has a short vowel sound.
  - *Open:* An open syllable ends in a vowel, and the vowel is long.
  - *Vowel-consonant-e:* A V-C-e syllable ends in one vowel, one consonant, and a final *e.* The final *e* is silent, and the vowel is long.
  - *Vowel team:* A vowel team is two vowels together that make a special sound.
  - *R-controlled:* Occurs when an *r* comes after a vowel that makes a special sound.
  - *Consonant-le:* A syllable ends in a consonant followed by the letters *le,* which make a separate syllable.

Written Language

- The three-step planning strategy for story writing is as follows (Harris & Graham, 1996):
  - Think (Who will read this? Why am I writing this?).
  - Plan what to say using SPACE (**s**etting, **p**urpose, **a**ction, **c**onclusion, **e**motions).
  - Write and say more.

- The story grammar strategy includes five steps (Harris & Graham, 1996):
  - Think of a story you would like to share.
  - Let your mind be free.
  - Who is the main character, and who else is in the story? When does the story take place? Where does the story take place? What does the main character do or want to do; what do the other characters do? What happens to the main character and the other characters when they do what they do? How does the story end? How do the characters feel?
  - Make notes of your ideas for each part.
  - Write your story.

- The WRITER strategy teaches students to do the following:
  - **W**rite on every other line.
  - **R**ead the paper for meaning.
  - **I**nterrogate yourself using COPS (see pp. 92–93).
  - **T**ake the paper to someone to proofread.
  - **E**xecute a final copy.
  - **R**eread your paper a final time.

Middle School

General Study Skills

- A strategy for helping students in classroom discussions is SLANT, which stands for (1) **s**it up, (2) **l**ean forward, (3) **a**ct as though you are interested, (4) **n**od, and (5) **t**rack the teacher (Ellis, 1989).
- Note-taking skills can begin with having students complete guided notes, which are partial notes or outlines given to students before the lecture or video with blanks or other places for a response. Students complete these partial notes during the lecture, and the class shares answers afterward. Students can also complete two-column notes with the concept or vocabulary on one side and examples or definitions on the other. They can also be taught the Cornell Note-taking System (different versions exist), which often includes a recall column, the notes column, and a summary.
- Provide instruction on how to use an assignment notebook, especially if middle school teachers expect students to write assignments differently than did elementary teachers.
- Have students complete a learning styles inventory or learning preference inventory (many are available online) and discuss how they may learn best.

Math

- Students can use graphic representations to solve problems by using visual aids and creating diagrams that organize the information in the story problem.
- The Solve It! strategy (Montague, 2006) includes these steps:
  - Read the problem for understanding.
  - Reread and paraphrase the problem.
  - Visualize and draw the problem.
  - Hypothesize a plan and write the problem.
  - Estimate the answer.
  - Compute and solve the problem.
  - Check the answer.

Reading Comprehension

- Reciprocal teaching is a cooperative learning approach that involves these four strategies:
  - *Summarizing:* Identifying and paraphrasing the main ideas
  - *Questioning:* Questioning oneself about the content
  - *Clarifying:* Discerning when there is a breakdown in understanding and identifying strategies to find meaning
  - *Predicting:* Hypothesizing the next event in the text
- Teach students how to adjust reading rate for different purposes.

Written Language

- Students can learn abbreviations for note taking and writing drafts.
- Teach students the PENS strategy:

P: Pick a sentence type (simple, compound, complex, or compound-complex sentence)

E: Explore (think of) words to fit the sentence type.

N: Note (write) the words.

S: Search (look for verbs and subjects) and check.

- Teach outlining skills for textbook reading and writing.

High School

General Study Skills

- *Marking the text:* Encourage students to use different symbols or colors for marking documents to indicate main idea, subtopic, detail, or sequence.
- *Review test-taking strategies:* Students may be able to narrow choices by using these five tips:
  - Generally, in a multiple-choice item, pick the longest or most detailed answer.
  - If you do not know the answer, pick option B or C, as these choices are most frequently the correct answer.
  - Eliminate answers that are very similar.
  - As you read the question, anticipate the answer and then look for that answer in the array of choices (Friend & Bursuck, 2006).
  - When in doubt, answer *true* for true-false items, as *true* is most frequently the correct answer.

- Have students identify how teachers indicate what is important. Some teachers write on the board, others speak more loudly, others use phrases such as "remember this" or "this is important."

Math

- For order of operations, the ORDER strategy includes these five steps:
  - **O**bserve the problem.
  - **R**ead the signs.
  - **D**ecide which operations to do first. (To remember the rules of operation, recall the sentence "**P**lease **e**xcuse **m**y **d**ear **A**unt **S**ally," for **p**arentheses, **e**xponents, **m**ultiplication, **d**ivision, **a**ddition, **s**ubtraction.)
  - **E**xecute the rules of order.
  - **R**elax—you are done.

- The FASTDRAW strategy helps students solve algebra story problems with these steps:
  - **F**ind what you are solving for.
  - **A**sk yourself: What information is given?
  - **S**et up the equation.
  - **T**ake the equation and solve it.
  - **D**iscover the variable and operations.

○ Read the question and combine like terms.
○ Answer the question or draw and check.
○ Write the answer for the variable and check the equation.

Reading Comprehension

- The SQRRR strategy steps are as follows:
  ○ *Survey:* Quickly look over the table of contents, chapter titles, headings, subheadings, figures, tables, and conclusions.
  ○ *Question:* Turn major headings and or subheadings into questions that serve as a purpose for reading.
  ○ *Read:* Read each section at a time, looking for answers to the questions from Step 2.
  ○ *Recite:* Recall the important points from the reading by saying or writing them.
  ○ *Review:* Review critical information.

Written Language

- The DEFENDS strategy is for writing theme papers and reports. The steps are as follows:
  ○ Decide on your exact position.
  ○ Examine the reasons for your position.
  ○ Form a list of points that explain each reason.
  ○ Expose your position in the first sentence.
  ○ Note each reason and supporting points.
  ○ Drive home the position in the last sentence.
  ○ Search for errors and correct.

■ WRITTEN LANGUAGE EDITING STRATEGIES

A number of effective written language strategies have been developed that may help Mr. Patel and Ms. Davis as they work with their students. Some of these are described below.

The COPS Strategy

The COPS strategy—also called the Error Monitoring Strategy (Schumaker, Nolan, & Deshler, 1985)—has been used, with variations, by general and special education teachers at different grade levels. This strategy teaches students to monitor, or proofread, their work for capitalization errors, overall appearance issues, punctuation errors, and spelling errors. The acronym COPS is used to help students remember the steps, and many elementary teachers provide a visual (picture or bulletin board) of a police officer with steps as a visual reminder.

The COPS strategy is best taught using teacher demonstration, with many subsequent opportunities for students to practice finding errors. The strategy steps are as follows.

C: *Capitalization*

In this step, students are taught to look at their written work *only* for capitalization errors and ask themselves (1) Have I capitalized the first word of the sentence? and (2) Have I capitalized all of the proper nouns in the sentence?

O: *Overall Appearance*

In this step, students look at their written work *only* to review its over-all appearance. They ask themselves (1) Is my handwriting easy to read, on the line, and not crowded? (2) Are my words and sentences spaced right? (3) Did I indent and write close to the margin? and (4) Are there any messy errors?

P: *Punctuation*

In this step, students proofread *only* for punctuation errors. The key proofreading questions include (1) Did I use the right punctuation mark at the end of each sentence (such as a period, question mark, or exclamation mark)? and (2) Did I use commas and semicolons where necessary? (If commas and semicolons have not been introduced in the curriculum, omit the second question.)

S: *Spelling*

The last step asks students to review their papers *only* for spelling errors as they ask themselves (1) Does the word look right? (2) Can I sound it out? and (3) Have I used the dictionary?

The steps of the COPS strategy are introduced one at a time with opportunities for students to master that step. After students have learned how to edit each of these components separately, they practice proofreading for all four items at the same time.

Structured Proofreading Strategy

Similar to COPS is a five-step structured proofreading strategy with these steps:

1. Check capital letters at the beginning of each sentence *only* and then return to the beginning of the passage.

2. Look *only* at end punctuation and then return to the beginning of the passage.

3. Proofread for capitalization of proper nouns *only* and then return to the beginning of the passage.

4. Look for sentence fragments and run-on sentences by using a four-step process (Birsh, 2005):
   o Check for and eliminate every *and.*
   o Insert a period and change the first letter of the next word into a capital.

o Read each group of words *aloud* to determine whether or not they constitute a complete sentence.

o Restore the *and*'s and eliminate the capital and period only where a group of words is correctly written as a phrase or clause.

Peer-Revising Strategy

Another strategy, which incorporates COPS but uses peers in the editing process, is a peer-revising strategy. A goal of many classrooms today is to develop a sense of community where all students are respected. One way of promoting student sharing and collaboration is through a peer-revising strategy, where peers react and make suggestions concerning each other's work. Harris and Graham (1996) note that this peer-editing process can be done through written feedback or in person by an individual, small group, or the class as a whole. They further maintain that the peer-revising strategy is effective for improving student editing because it makes the audience an integral part of the process.

The peer-editing process recommended by Harris and Graham (1996) includes two parts:

1. Revise

- Listen to the writer read his or her paper and silently read along.
- Tell what the paper is about and what you liked best.
- Read and make notes. Think about these questions: Is everything clear? Can any details be added?
- Discuss your suggestions with the author.

During this first part, each student is assigned a writing partner. After each student completes a first draft, writing partners get together and complete Step 1. One author reads his piece, while the other uses active listening skills and silently reads along to ensure she understands the piece. After the paper is read, the peer indicates what she liked best about the piece, starting the peer-editing process in a positive manner. She also tells what the paper is about to encourage understanding main ideas and details. Then authors exchange roles and begin the process again.

After these steps, each student reads the peer's paper to himself while asking (1) Is everything clear? and (2) Could details be added somewhere? He may ask the peer for clarification as needed. Students are encouraged to make at least three suggestions for the author and to write them right on the paper. Peers get back together to discuss their ideas. Each student makes suggestions for implementing the suggestions.

The second part of the strategy involves editing for specific errors. Before giving the paper back to their partners, authors self-edit using the questions in Step 2.

2. Proofread

- *Sentences:* Is each sentence complete?
- *Capitals:* Are the first letters of every sentence and of proper nouns capitalized?

- *Punctuation:* Does every sentence end with punctuation?
- *Spelling:* Circle words about which you are unsure and check the spelling with your word list, spell checker, or dictionary.

Students again exchange papers, and each independently uses the checklist to find and correct errors. Lastly, students get back together and discuss corrections before they write the next draft.

The Revise Strategy

A similar strategy, which can be used by the author alone or with a peer, is the Revise Strategy (Polloway, Patton, & Serna, 2005). The steps of this strategy are as follows:

1. Reread your paper to confirm overall goal is reached.

2. Edit using COPS.

3. Vocabulary selected to be appropriate for purposes.

4. Interesting and lively topic developed.

5. Sentences complete and varied.

6. Evidence provided to support your points.

TEACHER BEHAVIORS   ■

Regardless of their age or grade, while teaching study skills or strategies to students, we offer these suggestions:

- Begin study skills instruction in the lower elementary grades. A coordinated K–12 study skills curriculum provides an important framework for students, communicates to parents that teachers value study skills, and helps students transition to the next grade.
- Informally assess study skill usage, so you can pinpoint which study skills students are using and not using. A pretest will provide valuable information on which to base your instruction. Check student background knowledge as well as student misconceptions regarding study skills.
- Share a rationale with students about how the study skill or learning strategy will help them and results they may expect.
- Teach broad uses of the study skill. Many study skills and strategies can be used in many contexts. Grade-level teachers can collaborate on identifying study skills common to many disciplines and remind students to use them in many classes.
- If you are teaching a learning strategy with several steps, consider these steps (Harris & Graham, 1996):
  ○ Develop background knowledge.
  ○ Discuss the skill or strategy.
  ○ Model the strategy.
  ○ Have students memorize the steps of the strategy.

        ○ Support student use of the strategy with lots of practice.
        ○ Have students perform the strategy independently.

- Consider videotaping peers doing the study skill or strategy successfully to demonstrate it to the entire class. This approach has been especially effective when teaching the peer-editing process.
- Include a visual, checklist, form, or other cuing device for students. Some students need an additional way to remember steps. A cue sheet, poster, bulletin board, or checklist with steps serves as a helpful reminder.

■ BACK TO OUR TEAM

Our team is challenged by the fact that despite DOL activities and other worksheet and textbook practice assignments, fourth graders are submitting written work with numerous mechanical errors. This has upset Mr. Patel, and students are receiving low grades on their writing pieces. This has also upset Ms. Davis, who is finding that she does not enjoy co-teaching very much due to the stress.

Because of these issues and the realization that neither teacher is enjoying co-teaching as much as expected, Mr. Patel considers a plan that might work, and he presents this to Ms. Davis at an appropriate time. Mr. Patel decides to use a word picture (in combination with the sandwich technique) to communicate with Ms. Davis. A word picture is a communication technique that involves using a metaphor, simile, or analogy that "paints a picture" of the situation or concern. Because Ms. Davis is a golfer, Mr. Patel uses golfing in his word picture analogy. He decides to say something like the following.

Word Picture and Sandwich Technique Combined

Stephanie, I know how much you care about these students, and I appreciate your daily DOL work with them and your enthusiasm for teaching. As we grade their writing, though, we both see that many of these students are not generalizing skills presented during the daily DOL sessions. They need more instruction and practice than just the DOL we do at the beginning of each class. This is like when you learned to golf—you took lessons, practiced, received lots of feedback, and after all of that work and quite a bit of time, you became an accomplished golfer. I think our students' editing skills are like that—they are like novice golfers, and they need a coach. We are expecting them to hit a hole-in-one when most are below par when editing their writing.

Mr. Patel then shares an idea that involves providing more instruction—in the form of teaching a strategy. He indicates that perhaps a strategy that organizes skills within a single mnemonic framework would be easier for students to use and retain than remembering a lot of rules that are difficult to generalize. He indicates that this strategy can be presented over several days, so the class will still have time for reading and spelling. Mr. Patel indicates that he would like to see if teaching students the COPS strategy will help them generalize their editing skills, so they can eventually do peer editing, which is one of the fourth-grade language arts outcomes.

The Result

Ms. Davis agrees to the plan. Starting Monday, the co-teachers will shift the emphasis from DOL activities to COPS strategy instruction. Because students have found editing boring and the co-teachers also want to do something different and add positive energy to their class, they decide to be creative in how they introduce the COPS strategy.

The team, therefore, decides to do some planning. Mr. Patel agrees to review his understanding of the COPS strategy by rereading his manual. He will model one step of the strategy each day for the next four days. He also shares ideas for teaching students to self-monitor using a COPS check-list, and he presents a bulletin board or poster idea that provides a visual reminder for students to use the COPS strategy. Ms. Davis agrees to develop interesting guided practice and independent practice activities different from the worksheets students have already completed. She will develop passages at the students' independent reading levels that can be used for these purposes, and she will use names from the community (stores, etc.) to add interest to sentences and stories. The team decides to use some team teaching during parts of their lesson.

Instead of introducing the lesson in a typical manner, the co-teachers decide to do some role-playing as part of their lesson introduction. Ms. Davis agrees to create the dialogue and e-mail it to Mr. Patel over the weekend for his input and review. As the team leaves, they are feeling better about their professional relationship and their class. They have selected a research-based approach, and they are adding some novelty and creativity to their lesson that would be difficult to do with just one teacher. Both leave their meeting optimistic about their future co-teaching endeavor, and each teacher has specific responsibilities for preparing for this new approach. While sharing his concern, Mr. Patel never blamed Ms. Davis. He kept the discussion focused on how best to teach students.

LESSON PLAN   ■

Day 1

Advance organizer: Short role-play with Ms. Davis (as teacher) and Mr. Patel (as student). Ms. Davis begins: "Let me have your attention, class. Watch and listen to see if anything like this has happened to you." The team role-plays a teacher returning papers to students. Mr. Patel is excited about receiving his paper, and he expects a good grade because he thought his ideas were really creative. Instead, he sees a C– on his paper with many items circled, and he shares his disappointment. He concludes, "No matter how hard I try, I get bad grades on my papers."

Introduction to strategy: The teachers then step out of their role-play and discuss with the class why the student received the poor grade, if that has ever happened to them, and why mechanics are as important as content. The team introduces the COPS strategy, provides a rationale for learning this strategy, and shares results other students have achieved after learning this strategy.

Initial instruction: Mr. Patel introduces the *C* step of the strategy, which includes the two questions (1) Have I capitalized the first word of the sentence? and (2) Have I capitalized all proper nouns in the sentence? As he introduces these questions, Ms. Davis posts these two questions (prewritten on construction paper) on a bulletin board visible to all students. She reviews the difference between nouns and proper nouns with a class discussion, examples and nonexamples, and a short activity. To prepare for the activity, while Ms. Davis reviewed with the class, Mr. Patel quietly distributed two note cards to each student: one with the letter *N* and one with the letter *P*. The activity involves all students. As one co-teacher says a word that is a noun or proper noun, students hold up the *N* card if the word is a noun and *P* if the word is a proper noun. This activity promotes unison responses, active involvement, and immediate teacher and student feedback.

Modeling: Next, Mr. Patel models how to use the *C* questions with a short passage. He presents the passage on the overhead, orally reads it sentence by sentence, and asks himself after every sentence (1) Have I capitalized the first word of the sentence? and (2) Have I capitalized all proper nouns in the sentence? He finds several errors, and he corrects them with an overhead marker.

Guided practice: After asking students if they have any questions, Ms. Davis explains the guided practice activity, which is a different passage with eight capitalization errors. With their partners, students find and correct all eight errors. Students work in pairs as both co-teachers circulate and observe and assist. The class goes over the answers.

Independent practice: Ms. Davis presents a different passage for a short homework assignment that is due tomorrow.

Closure: Mr. Patel asks the class to state the two questions in the *C* step of the COPS strategy before they begin they transition to the next language arts activity.

Day 2

Review: Day 2 begins with a quick review of the *C* step and the difference between nouns and proper nouns.

Advance organizer: Short role-play with Ms. Davis (as teacher) and Mr. Patel (as student). As Mr. Patel is preparing to hand in his paper, he says to himself that he needs to use the *C* step to make sure he capitalized the first word of every sentence and every proper noun. He orally reads his short paper and is pleased with his capitalization corrections. "I am ready to hand in my paper," he declares. Ms. Davis takes his paper and places it on the overhead for everyone to see. His paper is a mess; complete with smudge marks, cross-outs, and little pictures in the margins.

Ms. Davis asks the class, "Do you think this paper will earn a good grade?" Then, the role-play concludes.

Initial instruction: Both teachers allow students to answer Ms. Davis's question. The class discusses the importance of a neat paper that creates a positive first impression.

Modeling: Mr. Patel introduces the *O* step, which stands for "overall appearance." With the messy paper already on the overhead, he asks himself these critical questions one at a time: (1) Is my handwriting easy to read, on the line, and not crowded? (2) Are my words and sentences spaced right? (3) Did I indent and write close to the margin? and (4) Are there any messy errors? While asking these questions, he points to and circles each error on his paper. "This will remind me to address this issue in my final draft," he notes. As he models each step, Ms. Davis adds those steps to the bulletin board.

Guided practice: After asking students if they have any questions, Ms. Davis introduces the guided practice activity. Again, students are given a passage with many overall appearance errors. Working with partners, they circle errors and identify the error category (handwriting, spacing, indention, or messy). As students find errors, both co-teachers circulate and answer questions. Students share their answers with the class.

Independent practice: Ms. Davis presents a different passage for a short homework assignment that is due tomorrow.

Closure: Mr. Patel asks the class to state what *O* stands for in the COPS strategy and list the four questions associated with this step.

Figure 6.1   Birthday Invitations

Invitation # 1

Dear Parent,

Your child is invited to Billy's birthday party. At our home, we will meet at 1:00 PM. At the park, we will play games at 2:00. At the Pizza Palace, we will eat at 3:00. At the zoo, pick up your child at 4:00. We think this will be fun for all! The snacks the children will eat—including the cake—will be provided. From you, we need an RSVP as soon as possible. Bring a gift if you like, but it is not required. Call 555-555-5555 to confirm.

Invitation # 2

Dear Parent,

Your child is invited to Billy's birthday party at our home. We will meet at 1:00 PM at the park. We will play games at 2:00 at the Pizza Palace. We will eat at 3:00 at the zoo. Pick up your child at 4:00. We think this will be fun! For all, the snacks the children will eat—including the cake—will be provided from you. We need an RSVP. As soon as possible, bring a gift. If you like, but it is not required, call 555-555-5555 to confirm.

Day 3

Review: Day 3 begins with a quick review of both the *C* and the *O* steps.

Advance organizer: Ms. Davis presents two birthday party invitations that have the same words yet are punctuated differently. Before she presents these on the overhead and orally reads them, she asks students to listen as she reads and shows each invitation. She asks the class to think about how punctuation makes a difference in these two invitations.

Initial instruction: After a short discussion on the difference in the two invitations and the importance of punctuation, Ms. Davis presents the third step of the COPS strategy, which is *P* for "punctuation."

Modeling: Ms. Davis introduces the questions involved with the *P* step. Those questions include (1) Did I use the right punctuation mark at the end of each sentence (such as a period, question mark, or exclamation mark)? and (2) Did I use commas [and semicolons] where necessary? (Because this class has not learned semicolons, she omits that part of the strategy.)

Earlier, Mr. Patel informed Ms. Davis that the class received instruction on using commas to separate (1) items in a series, (2) parts of a compound sentence, (3) cities and states, and (4) various items in a letter such as the greeting and closing. With a passage on the overhead with numerous punctuation and comma errors, Ms. Davis then models, using self-talk and self-questioning, how to correct the piece. She makes the corrections in color using an overhead pen. As Ms. Davis models each step, Mr. Patel adds those steps to the bulletin board.

Guided practice: After asking students if they have questions, Mr. Patel introduces the guided practice activity. Working in pairs, students are given a passage with many end punctuation and comma errors. They circle errors and make corrections. As students find errors, both co-teachers circulate and answer questions. Students share their answers with the class.

Independent practice: Mr. Patel presents a different passage for a short homework assignment that is due tomorrow.

Closure: Ms. Davis asks the class to state what *P* stands for in the COPS strategy and list two questions to ask during this step.

Day 4

Review: Day 4 begins with a quick review of the *C, O,* and *P* steps.

Advance organizer: The co-teachers perform another short role-play to capture student interest. Mr. Patel role-plays receiving a letter in the mail that declares he is the winner of a sweepstakes. He excitedly opens the envelope and starts to read the letter. He places the letter on the overhead for all students to see. As he begins to read, he stops, stumbles over words, and attempts to sound out some words because many words are misspelled. Finally, in frustration, he stops reading and crumples the letter and throws it away. The role-play concludes as Ms. Davis asks: Why did Mr. Patel throw that letter away? What impression did the writer leave with the reader? Why is correct spelling important?

Initial instruction: Ms. Davis transitions into introducing the final step of the COPS strategy, which is *S* and stands for "spelling."

Modeling: Ms. Davis introduces the questions involved with the *S* step, which are (1) Does the word look right? (2) Can I sound it out? and (3) Have I used the dictionary? Both teachers agree to modify Step 3 to be (3) Have I used the dictionary, spell checker, partner, or adult?

With a passage on the overhead showing numerous spelling errors, Ms. Davis models how to correct the piece using self-talk and self-questioning. She makes the corrections in color using an overhead pen. As she models each step, Mr. Patel adds those steps to the bulletin board.

Guided practice: After asking students if they have any questions, Mr. Patel introduces the guided practice activity. Working in pairs, students are given a passage with many spelling errors. They circle errors and make corrections while both co-teachers circulate and answer questions. Students share their answers with the class.

Independent practice: Mr. Patel presents a different passage for a short homework assignment that is due tomorrow.

Closure: Ms. Davis asks the class to state what *S* stands for in the COPS strategy and list three questions associated with this step.

Day 5

On this day, the class practices all the steps in the strategy together.

The co-teachers have presented all the steps of the COPS strategy, students have practiced those steps in pairs and through homework assignments, and the bulletin board has all the steps listed on it. Today, the teachers present a way to use all the COPS steps. Homework assessments indicate that students are ready for this material.

Review: Day 4 begins with a quick review of the *C, O, P,* and *S* steps.

Advance organizer: Mr. Patel asks the class for examples of being able to complete the separate steps of a job or skill but not being able to put those steps together. For example, you might be able to complete each step in a three-digit division problem, but you get confused when you have to do all of the steps at once.

Initial instruction: Ms. Davis notes that the COPS strategy might be like that: "The acronym COPS and the bulletin board will help you remember the steps until they are automatic, but the strategy requires you to complete each step accurately and smoothly."

Modeling: The co-teaching team role-plays all steps correctly for students. They assume the role of a fourth grader writing a science report. With the first rough draft on the overhead, Ms. Davis models the *C* step, then Mr. Patel models the *O* step, and so forth until all steps have been completed. As the co-teachers model their strategy steps using self-talk and self-questioning, they also check off each question on their self-monitoring sheet, shown in Figure 6.2.

Guided practice: After asking students if they have questions, Mr. Patel introduces the guided practice activity. To add some variety, today the guided practice will be similar to the DOL the class has done in the past.

Figure 6.2 COPS Checklist

Name: _____

Directions: Proofread your paper using the steps of the COPS strategy. Place a ✔ in each box after you have edited your paper using that step.

COPS Element	Have I . . .	Check ✔
Capitalization	Capitalized the first word of every sentence?	
Capitalization	Capitalized all proper nouns in every sentence?	
Overall Appearance	Made sure my handwriting is easy to read, on the line, and not crowded?	
Overall Appearance	Made sure my words and sentences are spaced right?	
Overall Appearance	Indented and written close to the margin?	
Overall Appearance	Cleaned up messy errors?	
Punctuation	Used the right punctuation mark at the end of each sentence?	
Punctuation	Used commas correctly?	
Spelling	Looked at all the words to see if they look like they are spelled correctly?	
Spelling	Tried to sound out words that are hard to spell?	
Spelling	Used the dictionary, spell checker, partner, or adult to help me spell words correctly?	

Students come up to the overhead and locate, circle, and correct errors. Both co-teachers are active in asking students key questions such as these: What is the next step? What questions do we ask ourselves?

Independent practice: Mr. Patel presents a different passage for a short homework assignment that is due tomorrow. Students are presented with a COPS checklist along with this homework assignment. They will use their checklist to check off each completed step.

Closure: Ms. Davis asks the class to state what COPS stands for and the questions in each step. The class responds together.

■ COPS AND OTHER CO-TEACHING MODELS

This example illustrated the use of some team teaching with the COPS strategy. At various instructional points, both teachers were leading, questioning students, and adding to the other's perspective. The remaining co-teaching models could also be used, as noted on page 103.

- *One teach, one observe:* As one teacher is taking the lead, the other teacher could observe student behaviors and reactions to the lesson presentation with the goal of determining how long students in the class can attend to teacher modeling without losing interest. This information would be helpful as the teachers plan future lessons.
- *One teach, one drift:* While the partner is providing instruction and modeling skills, the co-teacher could circulate to ensure that students are paying attention. Especially during small-group work and independent work, one teacher could drift to answer student questions, perform a quick visual check of student work, guide them if errors are being made, and in general be proactive regarding behavioral or learning issues.
- *Station teaching:* After they have modeled the strategy, the teachers could develop learning stations with various proofreading activities. One station would have capitalization activities, while another would have punctuation activities, and so on. Students would rotate among these learning stations to gain more experience applying editing skills. Each co-teacher could supervise one station.
- *Alternate teaching:* Some students may already have mastered the basic editing skills taught in COPS. These students could be grouped for enrichment activities. Perhaps they are ready to learn more advanced editing skills, such as colons or semicolons, or perhaps they would enjoy learning the editing symbols used by journalists.

SUMMARY ■

This chapter presented information on teaching study skills and learning strategies with an emphasis on the COPS strategy, a research-based written language editing strategy that can be taught to students of all ages in all types of classrooms. Study skills and learning strategies help students be more independent. In a co-taught classroom, teachers can plan innovative and creative ways to introduce learning strategies, such as through role-plays as illustrated in this chapter. This chapter also presented the word picture, a verbal communication technique that uses an analogy, simile, or metaphor to communicate a need or issue.

REFLECTIONS TO APPLICATION ■

As co-teachers, have we . . .

- Examined our students' current use of study skills and learning strategies?
- Discussed reasons for incorporating study skills and learning strategies into the curriculum?
- Provided examples of various study skills and learning strategies to our students?
- Infused study skills and learning strategies into our instructional routines?

■ ADDITIONAL RESOURCES

Books

Davis, L., Sirotowitz, S., Parker, H., & Dimatteo, R. (1996). *Study strategies made easy: A practical plan for school success.* Plantation, FL: Specialty Press.

Graham, S., MacArthur, C. A., & Fitzgerald, J. (Eds.). (2007). *Best practices in writing instruction.* New York: Guilford Press.

Reid, R., & Lienemann, T. O. (2006). *Strategy instruction for students with learning disabilities.* New York: Guilford Press.

Web Sites

ACT, Inc. (2007). *Tips for the ACT multiple-choice tests.* Retrieved June 21, 2007, from http://www.actstudent.org/testprep/tips/subtests.html

Deshler, D. (2007). *A subtle, yet significant, name change* [Strategies Intervention Model]. Retrieved September 2, 2007, from the University of Kansas at Lawrence Web site: http://www.ku-crl.org/library/misc/name_change.shtml

Curricula and Other Texts

Archer, A., & Gleason, M. (2006). *Advanced skills for school success.* North Billerica, MA: Curriculum Associates.

Hughes, C. A., Schumaker, J. B., Deshler, D., & Mercer, C. (1988). *The test-taking strategy.* Lawrence, KS: Excellent Enterprises.

Minskoff, E., & Allsopp, D. (2003), *Academic success strategies for adolescents with learning disabilities and ADHD.* Baltimore, MD: Paul H. Brookes.

Schlemmer, P., & Schlemmer, D. (2007). *Teaching beyond the test book and CD-ROM.* Minneapolis, MN: Free Spirit.

Stebick, D. M., & Dain, J. M. (2007). *Comprehension strategies for your K–6 literacy classroom.* Thousand Oaks, CA: Corwin Press.

Wilson, D. W., & Wilson, R. A. (1997). *Improving study and test-taking skills: Grades 5–8+.* Greensboro, NC: Mark Twain Media/Carson-Dellosa.

Parent Resources

Brier, N. (2007). *Motivating children and adolescents for academic success.* Champaign, IL: Research Press.

Falvey, M. A. (2005). *Believe in my child with special needs: Helping children achieve their potential in school.* Baltimore, MA: Brookes.

Shay Schumm, J. (2005). *How to help your child with homework: The complete guide to encouraging good study habits and ending the homework wars* (rev. ed.). Minneapolis, MN: Free Spirit.

Wright, P., & Wright, P. (2006). *Wrightslaw: From emotions to advocacy—The special education survival guide* (2nd ed.). Hartfield, VA: Harbor House Law Press.

7

Teaching So They Are Engaged

Co-Teaching Using Student Involvement

Co-teachers Mr. Khan (general educator) and Ms. Alverez (bilingual teacher), both veteran teachers with master's degrees, are in their second year as co-teachers of this sixth-grade general education math class of 26 students, which includes 13 students with math IEP goals, 3 with 504 plans, and 4 who are English-language learners. Mr. Khan has been teaching for 25 years, and Ms. Alverez has been teaching for 18 years in the district and has recently earned her bilingual special education approval.

Mr. Khan begins class with an established routine, which is a written math problem on the overhead. He provides students with several minutes to read the problem, arrive at the answer, and show their work. After a few minutes, Mr. Khan asks for the solution. Several students raise their hand, and Mr. Khan calls on students until someone provides the correct answer.

Next, homework is checked as a class. Mr. Khan refers to a problem number and asks for the answer. Several students raise their hands, Mr. Khan calls on a student, and if the answer is incorrect, Mr. Khan proceeds to another student. After students check their homework, Mr. Khan demonstrates a new concept. After he demonstrates, students begin homework.

As students work problems, Ms. Alverez circulates, checks students, offers assistance, and reteaches as needed. The entire time, Mr. Khan has control of the class. The class is quiet and orderly with minimal behavioral issues. Students appear to be engaged and working.

In spite of the surface calm, Ms. Alverez has some concerns. When checking homework, she realizes that many students do not understand the concept, cannot verbalize what they are doing, and do not know how to apply the steps presented by Mr. Khan. During resource support at the end of the day, Ms. Alverez's fears are confirmed. Most students do not understand the concept, nor are they able to *complete their math homework. Ms. Alverez wonders if other students in the classroom learned the concept or if they are all having the same difficulty.*

Ms. Alverez feels that students need to be more actively engaged during the math lesson. She feels they need opportunities to receive immediate feedback. However, she is concerned about disturbing the calm, quiet, orderly environment established by Mr. Khan, who has been teaching this way for years. How will he react to suggestions that change is needed?

This team in a nutshell:

Grade level: 6

Classroom contextual factors: Diverse general education math classroom

Subject: Math

Co-teaching stage: Compromising stage, moving to collaborative

Interpersonal issue: Initiating change

Instructional challenge: Students are well behaved but not engaged

---

■ ACTIVE LEARNING

Active learning refers to techniques where students do more than listen and respond through paper and pencil. Active learning occurs when students are cognitively engaged in the subject matter. An active learning classroom can be recognized by a high rate of student activity, where students may be talking, writing, drawing, interacting, and questioning rather than sitting quietly or daydreaming. To create this setting, the environment needs to be nonthreatening and safe, so that students can practice skills and explore various ways to express their emerging knowledge.

This chapter focuses on using active learning strategies to empower and engage all learners. You will learn the importance of engaging all learners, as well as how to use various strategies. Specifically, after reading this chapter, you will be able to do the following:

- Identify ineffective strategies and summarize why they are ineffective.
- Define characteristics of active learning.
- Describe a variety of active learning strategies.
- Explain ways to incorporate active learning strategies in co-taught classrooms.

■ A RATIONALE FOR ACTIVE INVOLVEMENT

Teachers can consider several reasons for incorporating active learning techniques. First, scientific researchers have long known that human learning is more than just responding to stimuli, even if that stimulus is a motivating, engaging teacher demonstrating how to solve math problems. To learn, humans need to process information actively. Active engagement necessitates that students process their learning through activities such as talking, moving, writing, manipulating, and interacting. In short, learning can be a noisy, messy business in which students associate new knowledge with background knowledge.

Another reason to consider active learning is that the traditional model of instruction, where the teacher does most of the talking while students sit quietly absorbing facts, is inappropriate for diverse learners in today's classrooms. Today's students are used to a fast-paced, technology-driven way of life where information is quickly shared and exchanged. They see and hear megabytes of information via various media throughout the day. Similarly, national curriculum reports recommend that teachers reduce the amount of time students passively sit, listen, receive, and absorb information while they increase the time students actively learn, do, and collaborate.

Finally, when students are actively involved, teachers have important and ongoing assessment data on which to base instructional decisions. Active involvement allows students to display their knowledge, skills, and understandings throughout the lesson, so the teacher has data to support reteaching, reviewing, or advancing to the next skill.

TRADITIONAL INSTRUCTIONAL PRACTICES ■

Before describing active learning, we examine traditional instructional practices that do not engage all learners. Standard teaching practices are not bad or harmful, but they originated when the classroom was considered the melting pot and one-size-fits-all instruction was the norm. At the turn of the previous century, classrooms were the vehicle by which immigrants were homogenized into the American way of life. In today's classroom, well over a century later, teachers are confronted with great diversity and a mandate to teach each student.

Mr. Khan's classroom is an example of diversity experienced by teachers across the country. Students in diverse classrooms display a wide variety of background knowledge and experience, motivation, and learning, language, and attending abilities. Unlike teachers of the 1900s, today's teachers must engage all learners, in spite of vast differences in student skills, aptitude, attention, and motivation.

Even though expectations are different, many teachers today continue to use tools of homogeneity—the tools of the classroom of the previous century. These tools include hand raising and waiting to be called on; round-robin reading or answering; teacher-led instruction; and initiate, respond, and evaluate (IRE) questioning techniques. These instructional behaviors assume that today's classrooms are homogeneous.

Hand Raising

A very common, yet often ineffective, instructional practice is always requiring each student to raise a hand and wait to be called on. In fact, this practice is typically a classroom rule. Rather than engage students, hand raising actually encourages the disengaged to continue to disengage. While more assertive or knowledgeable students participate, what are other students doing? In many cases, they are disengaged, perhaps sitting quietly, either bored or daydreaming but probably not learning. All students must be actively engaged in the instructional conversation. Hand raising and calling on students, one by one, does not engage all students.

Blurting

Another ineffective classroom practice, similar to hand raising, is allowing students to blurt or shout out the answer. The blurter actually steals a learning opportunity from all other students, especially students who need more processing time. On the surface, most teachers discourage this practice, and they may even admonish the blurter. Many teachers, however, provide subtle approval to this practice by acknowledging the student or the correctness of the answer. Teachers, therefore, should reflect upon their classroom practices and note how they handle students who blurt out answers.

Sage on the Stage Teaching

Another common form of teaching in today's classroom is "sage on the stage" instruction (Feldman & Denti, 2004). *Sage on the stage* refers to an instructional practice in which the teacher spends the majority of class time presenting information by oral recitation, such as by talking or lecturing. The teacher is the "sage," sharing ideas for students to hear, process, and remember. Students who have strengths processing auditory information, organizing information, and storing information in long-term memory will succeed with this instruction. Students who do not understand complex oral language delivered at a rapid rate or who need to put information into their own words, work with manipulatives, or relate new information to their own experience will be less successful with this method.

Initiate, Respond, Evaluate (IRE)

IRE is another widely used practice in which teachers present questions and interact with students. The teacher initiates (I) the question, a student responds (R), and the teacher follows up with an evaluation (E) by saying either correct or incorrect. This format allows only one student at a time to respond. The teacher is viewed as the possessor of information to be poured into students' minds. The teacher does most of the talking. This questioning method restricts student involvement, because the teacher holds all the information and evaluates the correctness of students' answers.

Workbooks and Paper-and-Pencil Responding

Although workbooks may be a time saver for the teacher, as material is readily available in a systematic format, these instructional formats may be frustrating for learners in diverse classrooms. Often the font is too small, the language is too complex, the directions are inadequate, the range of examples is too limited, and the structured sequential practice is insufficient to ensure success. In addition, due to their limited understanding of the concept or fear of making an error, some students are threatened by writing permanent answers in their workbook or on paper. Further, using the same work book for the entire class illustrates one-size-fits-all instruction.

TYPES OF ACTIVE LEARNING ■

In contrast to instructional practices that involve only a few students, teachers can actively involve all students by using various strategies, such as choral or unison responding, thumbs-up responses, response cards, partner strategies, and classwide peer tutoring. These can be classified as group responses, partner responses, and individual written responses.

Group Responses

As the name implies, these responses involve the entire group to respond together.

Choral Responding

One type of group response is unison verbal responding or choral responding. This works best when there is only one correct answer and the answer is short. Choral responding provides a safe environment for applying new information. Students can either say the correct answer or make a judgment by giving a thumbs-up response.

The steps of this approach are as follows:

1. The teacher asks a question or makes a statement.

2. The teacher provides students with thinking time.

3. The teacher gives a clear visual or auditory signal indicating when students are to respond together.

4. Students respond together.

For this activity to be successful, students must be taught how and when to respond. Teachers do this by explaining the steps, modeling for students, and providing practice opportunities.

1. Provide a rationale and explain the activity. Say: "Class, we are going to learn a new way to respond. I know you all want to demonstrate that you know the answer, but if you raise your hands, I can only call on one person at a time, and the rest of you do not get an opportunity to share. So, instead of raising your hands, you are all going to respond together. I am going to ask a question, but I do not want you to say the answer. Instead, I want you to think about the answer. I will hold my hand up to indicate that you are to think. When I drop my hand, say the answer together."

2. Provide a model by showing and telling the steps. "Watch me do it: Step 1 is the question. The question is, 'What season is this?' Next, I am going to take a minute to think about the answer. I know this season is fall. Even though I know the answer, I am not going to shout it out. I am going to wait for the teacher's signal." [Model giving the signal.] "Fall."

3. Do the activity with the students while you provide a think-aloud. "Now you do it with me: I am going to start with something obvious, so you can practice the strategy and not worry about your answer.

"Here we go. Step 1 is I ask the question. The question is: What day is today?

"The next step is for you to think about the answer. Watch my hand; it is up, which means you need to be thinking.

"The last step is you give the answer together—but wait to answer until I give the signal. This time, I will drop my hand." [Drop hand.] All students respond together.

This strategy will only work if you teach the strategy thoroughly, provide practice, and provide a clear auditory or visual signal. In a co-taught classroom, one or both teachers can circulate around the room to ensure that all students respond.

Elementary Example

Miss Landen, a first-grade teacher, is teaching how to decode CVC words such as sad, nip, bum, etc. She displays words on an overhead projector, so she can watch the class while she touches the words. She touches the first word and says to students, "Look at this word. Sound out the letters silently as I touch each letter. After I touch each letter, I will tap the word. When I tap the word, say the word together. Remember, wait until I tap to say the word. Get ready. What word?" [Taps the word.]

Middle School Example

Mr. Khan is teaching his sixth-grade math students the place value of whole numbers and decimals. He has an overhead prepared containing various numbers. Mr. Khan touches a digit in the first number. He says: "Look at this number. Look at the digit I am touching. Think of the place value of this digit. When I tap the number, say the value of the place of this number. Get ready. What value?" [Tap digit.]

High School Example

In world history class, Mr. Knapp is reviewing the dates of various important battles. He says: "Listen, tell the year the Battle of Hastings was fought. When I drop my hand, say the year together. Think for a moment. Get ready: What year?" [Drop hand.]

Thumbs Up, Down, or Neutral

Another type of group response that provides students opportunities to respond without blurting is called thumbs up, down, or neutral. Thumbs up, down, or neutral can be used with questions that require students to process information more deeply.

In this group response, the teacher poses a question by juxtaposing two concepts. For example, in an elementary science class, the teacher might ask, "Can an inanimate object breathe?" Students indicate yes by putting their thumbs up and no by putting their thumbs down. If they do not know, they put their thumbs in a horizontal or neutral position.

To answer, students must carefully consider how the concept of *inanimate* is related to breathing. As students process the question and decide on their responses, the teacher can carefully watch all students to determine who has responded and who needs more instruction.

Examples of questions using this technique include the following:

- *Elementary example:* Does a mammal's body temperature change?
- *Middle school example:* Can a repeating decimal be divided evenly?
- *High school example:* Does the reverse of a function always exist?

This thumb-up activity can be followed immediately by the question: Why? Students can respond in writing using their dry erase boards (see section on written response). Be aware that developing questions requiring students to process information deeply requires much advanced thought. The questions cannot be developed at the last minute. Co-teachers working together can decide on the big idea of the lesson and determine how to construct questions related to the big idea to enable students to process deeply.

Thumbs Up When You Know the Answer

Thumbs up when you know the answer is another variation of group responding. Students are given a brief assignment, problem to work, section to read, etc. They are told to put their thumbs up when they have finished or when they know the answer. To avoid having arms waving in the air, before using this technique, demonstrate the correct way to give a thumbs-up signal. You may need to remind students each time or ask students to demonstrate an appropriate thumbs-up signal. The thumbs-up response allows students to demonstrate that they know the answer without blurting. If allowed to wave thumbs in the air, the benefit of this activity is defeated, and students requiring additional processing time are distracted and denied needed critical thinking time. As with previous activities, thumbs-up provides the teacher with a quick assessment of student knowledge. Before calling on a student, the teacher could circulate around the room and select a few students to whisper the answer to her or him.

The steps to this method are as follows:

1. Demonstrate how to give an appropriate thumbs-up response by keeping the fist planted on the desk and inconspicuously raising the thumb.

2. Provide an assignment, section of text to read, problem to work, question to answer, etc.

3. Provide a definite minimal amount of thinking time. Say, "I will wait at least one minute to check who has their thumbs up." (Indicate an amount of time that allows most students to complete the assignment.)

4. Avoid the void. "When you have finished, go back and reread to be sure you have found the correct answer." (Always provide an activity for students who finish quickly.)

5. Circulate around the room. Ask students with their thumbs up to whisper the answer to you. Provide corrective feedback if needed.

6. Check to see that most students have their thumbs up.

7. To avoid embarrassing any student, call on a student who whispered the correct answer to you.

Elementary Example

Rearrange manipulatives to demonstrate the place value of a variety of double-digit numbers.

Middle School Example

Change a fraction into a percentage to the nearest tenth.

High School Example

Read a passage from a content area textbook and determine the main idea or locate the topic sentence.

Cultural Considerations

Before using either of the thumbs-up active learning methods, be aware that in some cultures, thumbs up is considered an obscene gesture. To guard against inappropriate cultural practices, determine if any students come from a cultural background in which this gesture is considered obscene, take time to talk to them privately about how the thumbs up is used in our culture, and reconsider using these activities if the student's cultural background interferes with the use of this response.

Response Cards

Another variation of whole-group response is the use of response cards. Response cards can be used when a limited number of responses is possible. In this method, students are given or instructed to write responses on index cards or preprinted cards. The teacher poses a question, and students display the appropriate card. For example, in working on the homophones *to*, *too*, and *two*, students would write each word on a card, the teacher would say a sentence using one of these words, and students would display the correct card.

Elementary Social Studies Example

Students write the words *Greek* and *Roman* on separate index cards. The teacher mentions an historical figure, city, invention, or other contribution. Students hold up the name of the culture from which it came.

Middle School Math Example

Students write the words *tenths*, *hundredths*, and *thousandths* on separate index cards. The teacher writes a decimal on the overhead and asks the how the last number would be read. For example, for the number 32.089, students would display the thousandths card, and for the number 13.9, students would display the tenths card.

High School Civics Class Example

Students write each branch of government on a separate index card. The teacher names an activity, job title, or individual's name, and students hold up the correct corresponding card.

Partner Strategies

Another form of active engagement is structured partner work. This active learning strategy is appropriate for all age groups. There are, however, two caveats for effective partner activities:

1. Effective partner relationships must be created. Great care must be taken when teaming students to work in pairs. High-performing students should be paired with middle-performing students, and middle-performing students should be paired with lower-performing students.

2. Tasks must be clearly defined and modeled with definite steps.

Partner work enables students to interact with one another, share answers, and receive feedback before presenting their answers to the entire group. Students experience less pressure when they can discuss their answers with peers.

Think-Pair-Share (1–2–3)

1. Think

   a. The teacher provides students with a question to consider.

   b. The teacher provides a given set amount of time for students to "think" (usually about one minute).

   c. The teacher sets the timer for "think time."

   d. During think time, students may write their answers on a dry erase board, which keeps them focused and prevents an "I forgot!" response.

2. Pair

   a. Students are given a set amount of time to share their answers with their partners—usually two minutes.

   b. Partner teams are given a task such as "Prioritize your answers," or "Determine the best answer to share with the group."

3. Share

   a. Student pairs are called on to share their answers with the whole class.

   b. When teachers ask, "What did you and your partner think?" no student is embarrassed for not knowing the answer.

   c. The timer can be set for three minutes to keep the activity moving.

Share Variation

A variation of the think-pair-share can be used when students are brainstorming lists within a category. After the pairing section but before the sharing section, the teacher requests that partners prioritize their answers, indicating either one, two, or three. Partner groups share their best answer with the group. If that answer has already been mentioned, then the pair must select a different answer. Because groups cannot mention an answer another group has given, all groups remain focused as each pair gets to respond.

Elementary Example

Think of as many verbs as you can that can be used to replace the word *said*.

Middle School Example

Write as many prime numbers as you can think of.

High School Example

Think about a character in a novel or play you just read. Write down distinctive characteristics of that character. Support your thoughts with references to the text.

Classwide Peer Tutoring/Peer-Assisted Learning

A variation of partner work is peer tutoring and peer-assisted learning. Often, teachers like Mr. Kahn and Ms. Alverez tend to teach to a small set of average-achieving students. Unfortunately, as the scenario at the beginning of this chapter demonstrates, such whole-group instruction without differentiation may not meet the needs of many students in diverse classrooms. Researchers at Peabody College of Vanderbilt University have designed a method in which instruction can be decentralized, with students working with partners at their skill level. Their program is called Peer-Assisted Learning Strategies (PALS) for reading and math. The math program is intended to be used with students in Grades 2 through 8. The reading program can be used through high school. In both programs, a student is partnered with another student from an adjacent achievement level.

In PALS math, the two basic learning procedures include coach and player, and tutoring sessions last 25 to 35 minutes at least twice a week. Each tutoring session is reciprocal, so every student is both coach and player in the same session. The stronger student is the first coach. During coaching sessions, students work on a sheet of math problems in their area of math need (adding, subtracting with regrouping, number concepts, charts, graphs, etc.). While the player works the problems, the coach asks a series of questions designed to help guide the player through the problems toward skill comprehension and mastery. Midway through the tutoring session, students switch roles.

PALS reading is intended to target reading fluency, accuracy, and comprehension. Students are ranked in order from strongest to weakest readers, and then the group is split in half. The top-ranked reader in the high-performing half of the class is paired with the top-ranked reader in the lower half of the class. The second reader from the top-ranked half of the class is matched with the second reader from the lower half of the class. Matching continues in this manner until all students have been paired.

Each student pair is given a text to read. The entire class, however, does not read the same material. Reading material selected is based on the reading level of the weaker reader. Both members of the pair read the same text. The stronger reader is designated as the first reader and orally reads for a designated amount of time, typically five minutes. The weaker reader serves as the tutor. Then the weaker reader orally rereads the same material. Because the weaker readers read a text they have already heard, they are more likely to read accurately and fluently.

After each student has read a text section, he retells what he read in correct sequence. The tutor prompts by asking, "What did you learn first?" and "What did you learn next?" Following the retelling, partners engage in paragraph shrinking. In this activity, students work together to identify the main idea of each paragraph. They may also complete an activity called "prediction relay" to predict what they will read, read half a page out loud, and confirm or disconfirm their prediction.

Collaborative Strategic Reading (CSR)

A variation of partner reading designed to be used with content area texts at the middle school and secondary level is Collaborative Strategic Reading (Klinger, Vaughn, Dimono, Schumm, & Bryant, 2001). In this strategy, teachers introduce comprehension skills to use before, during, and after reading a section of a grade-level text book. Students work in pairs to apply strategies as they collaboratively read the text. They preview the day's reading assignment by asking each other what they already know about the topic and what they predict they will learn. They look at the title, subtitle, pictures, and captions to aid predictions. After reading a paragraph, they ask each other the main idea and important details. After reading the assignment, students restate the most important information learned that day and formulate questions they think the teacher will ask on a test. Throughout the entire session, students are actively engaged, reading at their own pace, selecting main ideas, and summarizing material they have learned. CSR is designed to maximize student involvement and enable all students to be successful in diverse general education classrooms. This activity can be used in any content area class at the third-through eighth-grade level and for intervention at the high school level.

Written Response

Dry Erase Boards

Another highly effective way to actively engage students is by using dry erase board written responses. Each student is given a lap-sized white board, dry erase marker, and dry erase eraser. The teacher poses a question, provides think time, and tells students to write the answer. As students write the answer, the teacher circulates and provides encouragement and corrective feedback, as needed. This step provides immediate feedback on students' knowledge. Many students are willing to write using a dry erase board rather than paper and pencil, because they can easily change or erase an answer. All students are held accountable for answering the question, rather than just the hand wavers. Teachers can observe which students are off-task or have not processed the question correctly. In addition, students get needed practice putting thoughts into writing. Dry erase boards can be used constantly throughout a lesson. The trick to their use is to have them immediately available and to make their use part a consistent part of your teaching repertoire.

Availability

Each student can be provided a dry erase board at the beginning of the year to keep in her desk. If you teach different groups of students each period, keep a class set of dry erase boards in a readily accessible part of your classroom. Tell students to get their dry erase boards at the beginning of class. Part of your class culture can be that being prepared means having your dry erase board, marker, and eraser ready when the bell rings, reducing transition time and increasing the likelihood of using this method.

Where to Obtain Them

Individual white boards can be purchased through a school supply catalogue or store. These tend to be small and rather pricey, though, especially if you purchase a class set. Another less expensive and more flexible way is to go to your local hardware superstore and ask for smooth white panel board. These come in large 8′ × 4′ × ¼″ sheets. For a small charge, the salesperson will cut the tile sheet into smaller sections to fit your desired dimensions. Keep your students' needs in mind as you decide what size to make the individual dry erase boards. You will need a size that is large enough for students to write on but small enough for them to handle. Middle school students seem comfortable with 18″ × 15″.

Markers and Erasers

Be sure to obtain low-odor markers. Request that students purchase their own or include three or four markers on the beginning-of-the-year school supply list. Teachers can purchase individual erasers, which are pieces of felt wrapped around a block of wood, but they are costly and easily lost. Instead of expensive erasers, students can use old socks or pieces of T-shirts, or students and teachers can purchase packages of colorful washcloths and cut them into fourths, which costs about $0.05 to $0.10 per student. Another inexpensive alternative is to use plastic sheet protectors, found at discount stores. Each student is provided with a plastic sheet protector. They write their response on the plastic cover and erase their response with a paper towel.

Teaching Behaviors

The challenge is getting into the habit of using dry erase boards Anytime you pose a question to the class, rather than have students raise their hands, have students use their dry erase board to write answers. Then circulate and observe what students have written.

Some examples of using dry erase boards:

- Think-pair-share: As mentioned earlier, have students write the "think" section of think-pair-share on their dry erase boards.

- Elementary math:
  - Write as many odd numbers as you can think of.
  - Draw the different ways 10 objects can be grouped evenly, 20 objects, etc.
  - Write as many different combinations of two numbers that can make 10.

- Middle school math:
  - Write the definition of a *prime number*.
  - Write this number on your dry erase boards: Nineteen and five thousandths, nineteen and five tenths, nineteen and five hundredths.

- Reading:
  - Use the dry erase board as part of CSR (mentioned earlier in this chapter):
    - Before reading a section from a content area textbook, have students preview the material by looking at the title, subtitle, pictures, and captions and predict what they might learn.
    - Have students brainstorm everything they know about a topic.
    - Unison read a paragraph or short section. Have students write the main idea on their dry erase boards.
    - When they have finished reading a section, challenge students to write a ten-word summary of what they have read.

- Grammar:
  - Display a sentence on the overhead matched to your students' reading level and interest. Choral read the sentence. Ask students to locate and then write the main verb on their dry erase board.
  - Display a simple sentence on the overhead, such as "Jack ran." Ask students to expand the sentence by adding adjectives, adverbial phrases, etc.
  - Display a picture on the overhead. Ask students to write three descriptive sentences about the picture.

Teachers have found several advantages to using dry erase boards. First, using dry erase boards allows teachers to respond immediately to students' learning needs yet hold them individually accountable for their answers. Workbooks only provide a limited amount of practice. Dry erase boards also allow teachers to adjust the practice level to students' needs. Dry erase boards can also be used to give all students the opportunity to answer higher-level questions safely, without fearing embarrassment. Teachers can also encourage students to process material more deeply by posing questions and requesting them to dry erase the answer. Finally, teachers who circulate and read student answers can provide individual positive or corrective student feedback. To avoid falling into the IRE question-answer trap, pose additional questions to enable students to process at a higher level. Some considerations include the following:

- Ask students to relate a concept to their own experience. "Where might you see this in your own life? Write some examples from your own experience."

- Ask students to rephrase or rewrite what someone else has said. "Put what Sam said in your own words. Write it on your dry erase board."
- Ask students to provide examples of a concept you have just taught. "Create your own problem that contains a repeating decimal."
- After reading a section of a novel or text, ask students to write questions they would ask the author, or "If you were writing the test, what test question would you develop?"

You can make positive comments individually to each student, as well as group comments such as the following:

- I notice that Mary has a unique response.
- Many of you have the same ideas.
- Mike has written five different questions he could ask the author.
- This part of your answer is correct, but you need to recheck what you have written here.
- Wow, this is a great idea that I have not considered!

Allowing students to express themselves in a nonthreatening manner through the dry erase board and making positive comments about their work increases active involvement in the lesson. This method also provides teachers with valuable information about what students know and what needs to be taught next.

■ BACK TO OUR TEAM

Ms. Alverez, the special education teacher, is concerned that students are not learning concepts. She has used interactive learning strategies when teaching small groups, but she is insecure about proceeding with a larger group. She is also concerned that her co-teacher is very structured and likes a quiet, orderly room. A communication tool Ms. Alverez could use in this situation is the *I* message.

I Message

"Mr. Khan, when I work with students at the end of the day, I notice that they do not seem to remember what we have presented in class. I am frustrated by this, because I have to reteach concepts we just presented earlier in the day. I have used some active learning strategies that seem to work very well in my small groups. I have never used these strategies with a group of 26 students. I wonder if we could try them in our math class. Perhaps we could divide the class into smaller groups to see if this strategy would work."

The Result

After discussing poor student daily homework and test scores and compromising to implement this method for a trial period, Mr. Khan and

Ms. Alverez decide to separate the class into two sections. This format provides Ms. Alverez an opportunity to teach half the class and become comfortable teaching a larger group than what she typically teaches. Ms. Alverez has been observing and supporting Mr. Khan's daily teaching, so she is familiar with the established routine, which they decide to keep while they use the parallel teaching model.

Parallel Teaching

The class is divided equally and randomly in two. Each teacher teaches the entire math lesson to half of the class. Each co-teacher teaches the exact same lesson, and both teachers incorporate active learning strategies into the established class routine. The co-teaching team decides to begin using peer-assisted learning, partner groups, and dry erase board responding.

At the end of the second week, the teachers change groups, while the groups remain the same. Mr. Khan takes Ms. Alverez's group, and Ms. Alverez takes the group previously taught by Mr. Khan. They continue this grouping pattern for another two weeks. By the end of four weeks, all students have engaged in active learning strategies with both teachers. Ms. Alverez has gained confidence teaching a larger group of students. Further, students have started requesting partner work and using dry erase boards because these "helped them learn."

LESSON PLAN ■

Before the co-teachers begin parallel teaching, they strategically divide the class into two smaller groups, ensuring that both sections are still heterogeneous. The team also develops lesson plans for the first few days and agrees to infuse various active learning methods each day. Here are the lesson plans each teacher uses for the three days using the parallel co-teaching model.

Day 1

As students enter the room, each teacher provides students with either a green or blue card, which will be used to divide students into instructional groups. Each teacher also has his or her own class list to ensure students do not trade cards with their friends. Before students move to their new places, both teachers explain the new grouping and active learning approaches they will be implementing. They emphasize that many of their established routines will not change but that students will be more involved in each class.

Review math problem on board: With their own group, each teacher presents a math problem on the board (as usual) for students to solve. Today's problem is a three-step story problem. However, instead of solving the problem individually, students use the think-pair-share approach. Students are familiar with this approach from their social studies class. After two minutes, students (in pairs) write their answers on their dry erase boards. Upon teacher cue, students reveal their dry erase boards for the teacher to see.

Check homework: The teacher says the problem number and the answer, and students check their own work and submit their papers.

Presentation of new concept: As usual, each teacher demonstrates the new skill for the day. The class begins a new chapter in the math book on data and graphs. To generate interest in this new unit, the teacher distributes a survey for each student to complete that asks the students to write their favorites, such as their favorite TV show, movie, song, class at school, etc. The teacher orally reads each question, and students write their responses on the survey. Indicating the goal to summarize class data, the teacher indicates that graphs or charts could be used to represent the class data. Today, the class will be making a frequency table and a line plot based on class data for the first two survey questions. The teacher asks each student to share his or her response to Question 1 and then Question 2. As students indicate their favorite TV show, the teacher makes a frequency table on the overhead and describes the steps. A similar process is used for student responses to Question 2—their favorite movie—as the teacher models and describes the steps involved in making a line plot.

Check for understanding: Before assigning homework, which is to make a frequency table and line plot based on data in the math text and answer questions about each, the teacher asks students questions about making the frequency table and the line plot: "What is our first step?" "What labels do we use?" "How do we know how many tallies to put in the frequency table?" "What is our favorite TV show?" "How many students indicated that (title) was their favorite show?" Students respond in unison.

Independent practice: Before students work independently, they use response cards (labeled "frequency table" and "line plot") to identify which data organization system is being described by the teacher. Finally, students begin their homework. The completed frequency table and line plot serve as visual models for students as they develop their own.

Dismissal and closure: Before dismissing the class and gathering student surveys, the teacher once more asks students questions about the process and products developed today. Students respond with the thumbs up, down, or neutral signs.

Day 2

Review math problem: As students enter, they see the review math problems on the overhead, which are pattern sequences. Students view three number sequences and complete the pattern. The teacher directs students to use the think-pair-share strategy for each pattern sequence and place their answers on their dry erase boards. At an appropriate time, students reveal their dry erase boards. While students are working on review problems, the teacher distributes yesterday's surveys to the students.

Check homework: The teacher presents homework answers on the overhead, and students check their own work.

Presentation of new concept: Today's skill involves making and interpreting bar graphs and line graphs. Referencing student surveys, the teacher calls attention to Question 3, favorite song, and Question 4, favorite class at school. Students share responses, and the teacher models and describes how to make a line graph based on data from Question 3 and a bar graph based on data from Question 4. At the conclusion of the demonstration, the teacher asks questions about the process of developing each graph as well as data in each graph, and students respond in unison.

Independent practice: Students use response cards labeled "line graph" and "bar graph" to identify which type of graph the teacher described. Then they begin their homework, which involves making a line graph and a bar graph and answering questions from the math text. The teacher's completed line and bar graphs serve as models. While students begin their homework, the teacher circulates and checks for accuracy.

Closure and dismissal: Before dismissing the class, the teacher reveals three questions on the overhead about today's product and process. Student pairs are asked to discuss each question verbally and come to agreement on their answers, and then they can put their materials away and be dismissed.

Day 3

Review math problem: The review math problem today involves comparing fractions using the <, >, or = sign. Students use the think-pair-share strategy.

Check homework: Students show and explain their work to their partners. They make any necessary corrections to their work before the teacher provides the answers on the overhead. Students correct their own work and submit their work.

Presentation of new concept: The new concepts today are *mean, median, mode,* and *range.* After preteaching these terms with examples, the teacher has students complete a roller coaster web quest (Wilcox, 2003) in the computer lab. The teacher places students in heterogeneous pairs and circulates to provide support.

Independent practice: The homework assignment is to complete several practice activities in the textbook on these concepts. The teacher's notes on the board serve as a visual reference for students as they begin their work. While students begin their homework, the teacher circulates and answers questions.

Closure and dismissal: Using response cards labeled "mean," "median," "mode," and "range," the teacher asks questions, and students hold up the corresponding card. Finally, the teacher dismisses the class.

OTHER CO-TEACHING MODELS ■

Other co-teaching models that could be used include the following.

- *One teach, one observe:* The one-teach, one-observe model could be used initially for one teacher to model active learning strategies for the other teacher. For example, Ms. Alverez could teach a lesson or part of a lesson using dry erase boards to model this technique for Mr. Khan.

- *One teach, one drift:* The one-teach, one-drift model could be used by this team by allowing Mr. Khan to drift around the room while Ms. Alverez models various active learning strategies.
- *Alternate teaching:* The co-teaching team could use alternate teaching when a few students demonstrate difficulty with a certain concept. While one teacher provides instruction for the majority of students, the other can take students to a different section of the room to provide additional practice.
- *Station teaching:* Station teaching is appropriate in math due to the various skills students learn in math and the emphasis on partner work. The co-teaching team could develop various stations that provide practice with recently presented skills. As a culminating review on fractions, for example, one station could review the addition of fractions while others offer practice simplifying fractions, finding the least common multiple, and so forth. To emphasize active learning, each station could involve students in a different way. One station could emphasize a peer-tutoring component, while another involves students working with a math software program and others require students to use their dry erase boards, perhaps under teacher supervision.
- *Team teaching:* The team could use team teaching as Ms. Alverez becomes more comfortable in front of the large group and as Mr. Khan becomes more comfortable with active learning strategies. In this approach, both present the lesson as a team, seamlessly moving between main teacher and support teacher roles. As they circulate, both teachers notice which students were learning and which need additional support.

◼ SUMMARY

This chapter focused on active learning strategies in co-taught classrooms. Active learning can be a very effective way to teach diverse learners. The chapter presented the characteristics of active learning and contrasted active learning with traditional classroom practices of hand raising, lecturing, and IRE question asking. The chapter described several effective strategies, such as group responses, partner responses, and dry erase boards. The chapter illustrated the *I* message as an effective communication tool to use with a co-teacher. Sometimes, indicating that an instructional change is considered a "trial" is helpful to those who resist change. At the conclusion of the trial, both teachers evaluate the appropriateness and success of the intervention. Finally, the chapter showed how active learning strategies could be used with each co-teaching model.

◼ REFLECTIONS TO APPLICATION

As co-teachers, have we . . .

- Examined our current practices regarding active engagement?
- Considered a variety of active learning strategies to use in our classroom?

- Evaluated and selected appropriate active learning strategies?
- Infused active learning strategies into our co-taught classroom?

ADDITIONAL RESOURCES ■

Books

Evanski, J. (2009). *Classroom activators: More than 100 ways to energize learners* (2nd ed.). Thousand Oaks, CA: Corwin Press.

Smokler, D. (2009). *Interactive learning experiences, grades 6–12: Increasing student engagement and learning* (2nd ed.). Thousand Oaks, CA: Corwin Press.

Walker Tileson, D. (2007). *Teaching strategies for active learning: Five essentials for your teaching plan.* Thousand Oaks, CA: Corwin Press.

Articles

Caulfield, J., Kidd, S., & Kocher, T. (2000). Brain-based instruction in action. *Educational Leadership, 58*(3), 62–65.

Kueker, D. (2005). Inviting students to the active learning process. *The Agricultural Education Magazine, 77*(6), 11–13.

Web Sites

Fuchs, D., Mathes, P., & Fuchs, L. S. *PALS: Peer-assisted learning strategies; Strategies for successful learning.* Retrieved November 21, 2007, at http://kc.vandcrbilt.cdu/pals/

8

Teaching So They Can Be Successful

Co-Teaching Using Formative Assessment

Meet Mr. Harris (third-grade general education language arts teacher) and Ms. Butera (special educator), who are third-year co-teachers. Both are veteran, tenured teachers with 12 years of teaching experience. Through her previous role as an inclusion facilitator, Ms. Butera frequently collaborated with Mr. Harris in designing and implementing accommodations for students with IEPs. These experiences helped her become acquainted with Mr. Harris's teaching and classroom management style and curricular areas. Mr. Harris learned to trust Ms. Butera as someone who could provide valuable insight into the learning needs of all students, not just those with IEPs. This experience working together proved invaluable as the team began co-teaching.

Before they started co-teaching, Mr. Harris covered the third-grade language arts curriculum with a combination of whole- and small-group instruction and supplemental activities. He used a grammar book, spelling book, basal reader, and grade-level chapter books. Based on standardized test scores, he placed students in skill-based reading and spelling groups. When he taught a small reading group, the remaining students typically silently read stories and answered questions or completed worksheet or workbook activities. He corrected these and recorded those scores in his grade book. Students took weekly spelling tests and occasional grammar tests. Student scores on these tests, as well as quizzes on reading stories and grades on written products, comprised students' final language arts grades. Students with disabilities typically received Cs or Ds in this class, because their writing skills and scores on these products were in the low-average range.

Over their three years as co-teaching partners, the co-teaching team has looked critically at curriculum, instruction, and assessments. In this process, they have *learned more about their students and their own approaches and philosophies about inclusive instruction.*

This team in a nutshell:

    Grade level: 3

    Classroom contextual factors: 24 students, diverse demographics

    Subject: Language arts

    Co-teaching stage: Collaborative

    Interpersonal issue: Different philosophies about grading

    Instructional issue: Students do not receive much corrective feedback about their work

---

FORMATIVE ASSESSMENTS ■

Observations, daily scores on assignments, error analysis, classroom reviews, and frequent short quizzes are examples of formative assessments. These types of assessments alert students about their ongoing progress in a skill area and provide data that informs day-to-day and moment-to-moment instructional decision making. Formative assessments provide feedback about the instructional effectiveness, the goal being for teachers to change what they teach and how they teach, if needed. Each student's achievement becomes the focal point. Rather than using assessment for the purpose of assigning grades, teachers continually ask themselves: Are all students in my class learning? If not, then I need to revisit and redesign what I am doing to ensure that all students are learning the essential material.

This chapter focuses on using various assessments, so you can teach purposefully. We emphasize the use of formative assessments. You will learn the difference between summative and formative assessments, how to design and use various assessments to improve the learning of all students, and the importance of collecting baseline data and conducting ongoing assessments. Specifically, after reading this chapter, you will be able to do the following:

- Describe the difference between summative and formative assessments.
- Describe the importance of using ongoing assessments to inform instruction.
- Collect data on students using curriculum-based assessments and curriculum-based measurement.
- Analyze a textbook's appropriateness based on students' reading levels.
- Use regular progress monitoring assessments to make instructional decisions.

■ THE WORLD OF ASSESSMENT

If you pick up a newspaper, listen to the evening news, or skim through the table of contents of many popular magazines, you will probably read or hear something about student test scores, high-stakes testing, and schools on the watch list. Perhaps more than any other time in history, largely as a result of No Child Left Behind (NCLB) and the Individuals with Disabilities Act (IDEA), teachers are being held more accountable for what they teach as evidenced by student test scores on district and state tests. Simpson, LaCava, and Sampson Graner (2004) note that NCLB is the most noteworthy of recent congressional attempts to improve student achievement and reform educational programs in the United States. Similarly, Albrecht and Joles (2003) indicate that NCLB serves as the most rigorous and exacting of standards-based strategies enacted for schools by mandating that all students demonstrate annual yearly progress.

Although tests required by NCLB and IDEA are important, teachers can include many other types of assessments in addition to administering end-of-the-year standardized tests. For example, they can incorporate a variety of formative assessments into their instructional routines. Typically, most assessments can be classified as either summative or formative.

Weekly spelling tests; pop quizzes; end-of-the-unit tests; midterm exams; final exams; local, state, and national high-stakes testing; and standardized tests such as those required by NCLB are summative assessments administered to evaluate learning at the end of a teaching unit or cycle; assign a grade; or determine if the student, school, or district has met targeted benchmarks. Summative assessments are accountability measures, but they do not improve student learning, nor do they provide information about student achievement in sufficient time for teachers to change instruction.

Formative assessments contrast with summative testing. Data from these assessments are used to improve student learning and provide teachers immediate information about the effectiveness of their instruction.

■ A RATIONALE FOR USING FORMATIVE ASSESSMENTS

One reason for using formative assessment is that the results directly inform instruction. Using frequently gathered student data as their guide, teachers can make changes in their instruction or curriculum to help students learn. The results of formative assessment provide decision-making data to teachers. Based on such data, teachers may review or reteach a concept or skill, move through parts of the curriculum at a different pace, or introduce skills in a different way. For example, a math teacher might reteach a math concept after analyzing student errors on a daily math assignment, or a language arts teacher might reteach parts of speech after noticing student confusion during a review session. Similarly, another teacher might advance through the curriculum more quickly or introduce more advanced concepts based on frequently gathered student data indicating student mastery. In short, data from formative assessment guides instruction like the captain at the wheel of a ship.

Secondly, formative assessment provides timely corrective feedback to students. Feedback is provided to students early enough to correct misunderstandings or faulty skills, thus preventing error learning from continuing. In other words, formative assessments help students learn. The most helpful types of feedback on tests and homework are specific comments about errors, specific suggestions for improvement, and comments that encourage students to focus their attention thoughtfully on the task rather than simply getting the correct answer (Bangert-Drowns, Kulick, & Morgan, 1991). Specific corrective feedback may be particularly helpful to students who are lower achieving, because it emphasizes they can improve as a result of effort. Formative assessment helps support the expectation that all children can learn to high levels and counteracts the cycle in which students attribute poor performance to lack of ability and, therefore, become discouraged and unwilling to invest in further learning (Vispoel & Austin, 1995).

A third reason for using formative assessment is that results can be motivating for students. Many students are encouraged and motivated when they see their math, reading, or spelling graph climb to higher levels. Even older students enjoy charting their progress and keeping track of their scores. A visual representation of improvement is more motivating to some students than a teacher's verbal praise, because students know that "data don't lie." In addition to teaching students to chart or graph their scores, teachers can help students set reasonable goals, which may help them become goal oriented and less reliant upon external reinforcement. These charts and graphs are also critical pieces of evidence to share during parent or student-led conferences.

EXAMPLES OF FORMATIVE ASSESSMENTS

Teachers can use various formative assessments depending on the grade level and subject. A few examples include the following:

Diagnostic pretests: Have students write or share their understanding of vocabulary or concepts before, during, and after instruction. One approach is to use K-W-L charts:

K: What do I know about this topic?

W: What do I want to learn about this topic?

L: What did I learn about this topic?

K-W-L charts and similar formats, such as anticipation guides (true-false statements that students answer before and then after instruction) are formative if the class revisits these frequently (at least three times during the unit) and revises responses based on new knowledge acquired during the unit.

Unit pretests: In content areas, such as science and social studies, unit pretests provide valuable information for teachers about students' entry-level knowledge and skills. Students who master the pretest can chose alternative and differentiated assignments rather than complete standard assignments.

Error analysis: Error analysis involves looking for error patterns, such as fact or algorithm errors in math; spelling, grammar, punctuation, sentence structure, or organizational errors in writing; reversals or incorrect letter sequence in spelling; comprehension or decoding errors in reading; and incorrect knowledge or misunderstanding of content in content areas. Rather than just checking an item incorrect, maintain a written record of the student's error (or teach the student how to do this) and analyze errors for patterns. Use student errors as an opportunity to reteach, remediate, or review. Help students learn from their mistakes; otherwise, students will likely repeat the same errors.

Miscue analysis: In reading, error analysis is often referred to as "miscue analysis." As the student orally reads, the teacher notes errors such as substitutions, omissions, reversals, repetitions, and insertions.

Homework and work sample analysis: This analysis involves looking for responses that indicate student misunderstanding or lack of skill in homework assignments or authentic permanent products. As with error analysis, teachers observe and classify error patterns and immediately reteach or correct student misunderstanding, so students do not repeat the same error.

Observation: Observation means watching students or groups as they solve problems, complete a lab or activity, or complete group work to determine ways in which they approach tasks. Admittedly, this is a challenge in classrooms led by one teacher. In co-taught classrooms, however, as one teacher leads instruction or attends to whole-group management issues, the co-teacher can observe and listen to particular students or groups to understand better the way they use language to mediate learning, the steps they take in solving problems, the types of leadership skills they demonstrate, and gaps or misunderstandings in background knowledge.

Written or verbal questionnaires and interviews: Interview students individually or in groups about their thinking as they complete authentic tasks associated with the subject. Co-teachers can share this responsibility, dialogue about their perceptions of students or groups, and decide how to differentiate instruction based on interview results. Interviewing students using structured formats, for example, may reveal that students are using different learning strategies or ways of thinking as they approach their work. Allowing students to share their strategies with others may benefit all learners.

Probes: Ask students to summarize quickly (verbally or in writing) the main ideas from a lecture, discussion, or assigned reading; assign a few problems or questions during the last few minutes of class with time to check answers; or have students complete timed tests on basic skills that provide a foundation for advanced skills, such as timed tests in math on multiplication facts. Although timed tests can be frustrating for some students, rather than competing with others, students can be encouraged just to improve their own score and compete with themselves. Lower elementary teachers often develop probes for solving basic math facts, identifying prefixes and suffixes, or other skills that students should develop at an automatic level. Secondary teachers can develop probes associated with big ideas and facts important in the content area.

One minute papers: Reserve one minute at the end of class for students to write a response associated with the big idea of the day's instruction (e.g., Why is this person or event representative of this period in history)? (Black & Wiliam, 1998).

3-2-1 papers: Provide a few minutes at the end of class or the week to have students respond to three prompts such as these: Write three things you learned. Write two things you identified with. Write one lingering question. A variation of the 3-2-1 paper is the RSQC2 format (Weber, 1999), which asks students to recall, summarize, question, comment, and connect by responding to these five questions: (1) Last class I learned . . . , (2) Today I learned . . . , (3) Today I questioned . . . , (4) During this class, I felt . . . , and (5) This lesson relates to . . . .

Rubrics: Using a scoring guide, such as a rubric, can provide assessment information as well as support student learning. A rubric should contain criteria, a measurement scale, and descriptions of the characteristics for successful completion of the assignment. By carefully designing a rubric, you clearly communicate expectations for student work or projects. You can also support student learning by using the rubric as a basis for providing ongoing assessment and feedback. By giving a clear indication ahead of time of what is expected and the range of scores assigned to each level of quality, the rubric becomes not only a guide through the assignment but also a systematic way for students to assess their own work. Rubrics are also very effective assessment instruments for diverse classes. By using a range of four or more gradations on quality, all students can be represented on the scale. Remember, though, that to be effective, rubrics must be well constructed and explicitly taught. An example of a writing rubric is shown in Figure 8.1.

DETERMINING THE STARTING POINT ■

In addition to using various formative assessments, teachers can consider the entering skills of each of their students relative to the concepts and skills they will be teaching. Next, they can determine if there is a match between each student's skill levels and the curricular material. To determine students' entry skills, our co-teaching team can use various informal assessments. For example, to determine the appropriateness of the textbook in relationship to their students' reading skills, they can use the cloze procedure, curriculum-based assessments, or the oral reading fluency (ORF) reading measure.

The Cloze Procedure

One way to determine if the textbook is written at the right difficulty level for students is to perform a cloze procedure. To prepare the cloze assessment, select a 250- to 300-word passage from an upcoming unit, story, or chapter. The first and last sentences are kept intact. Starting with the second sentence of the passage, replace every fifth word with a standard-length blank of about 10 to 15 spaces. (The blank line is always the same length, regardless of the length of the word it is replacing.) Delete 50 words in all. Students silently read the passage and fill in the blank spaces with the exact words without access to the print material. Figure 8.2 shows an example of a cloze assessment.

Figure 8.1   Rubic for Writing Assignment

Student:		Date:	
Essay:		Score:	

	Terrific (5)	*Good (3)*	*Needs more work (1)*
1. Grabber	Grabber is present and related to the main idea of the paragraph. Makes reader want to read more.	Grabber is present but not very strong.	Grabber is not related to the rest of the paragraph and confuses the reader.
2. Topic sentence	Topic sentence clearly states the main idea of the paper.	Topic sentence is simply stated.	Topic sentence does not clearly state main idea.
3. Sentence structure	Variety of sentences are used throughout, including these: • Complex sentences • Expanded simple sentences with adverbs, adjectives, and complex verbs • Sentence format is varied (not all sentences start the same way). • No grammar errors	Some of the sentences are varied, but most sentences use the same format. Some adverbs and adjectives are used. Almost no grammar errors.	Only simple sentences are used. Most sentences start the same way. No adjectives or adverbs used. Too many grammar errors. Too many "*ands.*"
4. Vocabulary	Many mature and descriptive words used appropriately.	A few mature words used appropriately. Or: Some mature words attempted but sound awkward.	Only basic words used; no mature words used. Or: Too many "empty words" like *thing, stuff,* etc.
5. Details	Each main idea has at least three details. All main ideas receive the same support. All main ideas supported with evidence, examples, or explanation.	Some main ideas have more support than others. Some use of evidence, examples, or explanation.	No use of evidence, examples, or explanation to expand ideas.
6. Transition	Mature transition words used appropriately. Ideas flow easily.	Simple transition words with some repeated. Ideas are easy to follow.	Misuse of transition words. Ideas are difficult to follow.

	Terrific (5)	Good (3)	Needs more work (1)
7. Title	Title is present and cleverly worded. Title is appropriately capitalized.	Simple title is present and appropriately capitalized. All words spelled correctly.	Title has errors in spelling or capitalization, or title is confusing.
8. Conclusion	Concluding sentence is present. Conclusion corresponds to the topic sentence. Closing ends the paper and ties the paper together. Makes reader think	Concluding sentence is present and is simply stated.	Concluding sentence is awkward. Reader does not know the paper is over.
9. Mechanics	No misspelled words. No punctuation errors. No capitalization errors. Paper is typed in correct-size font and double-spaced.	Only one or two spelling, punctuation, or capitalization errors. Paper is neatly handwritten.	More than two mechanical errors. Or: Paper is not neatly written.

Figure 8.2   Example of Cloze Assessment (Abbreviated Form)

Factors that influence an economy:

The process of producing, buying, and selling goods and services is called an economy. Some workers produce items _____ other people want to _____. Workers may produce vegetables _____ clothing or nails. Other _____ provide a service. They _____ fix a broken machine _____ they may be an _____ in a store who _____ clothing or food. People _____ the products or services _____ the worker. Sometimes people _____ directly from the worker, _____ sometimes a store owner _____ provide a service by _____ items from the worker _____ then reselling them to _____ people.

The agricultural economy _____ the United States met _____ of the basic food _____ of the people in _____ 13 colonies. However, the _____ also wanted manufactured goods _____ farmers could not produce, _____ as candles and tools. _____ craftspeople made some of _____ manufactured goods by hand.

_____ was the start of _____ manufacturing economy in the _____ States. Because there were not many craftspeople in the colonies, the colonists had to import most of the manufactured goods that they wanted.

Interpretation of Cloze Results

Students who achieve 60 percent or better selecting the exact word are at the independent reading level for the text. This means the text could be assigned for homework without any additional teacher assistance or instruction. For students who score between 40 and 59 percent, the text can only be used with ongoing teacher support. For students who score less than 40 percent, the text is too difficult and should not be used for independent reading. The cloze method provides teachers with a general sense of the match between the textbook and student reading skills, but students often are frustrated by this activity, and some authors question the reliability and validity of this measure. Therefore, we recommend using the cloze method in combination with other informal assessment measures.

Curriculum-Based Assessments

Curriculum-based assessments (CBAs) directly measure student performance in the local curriculum. These assessments are based on the assumption that teachers should directly test what they teach. Some examples of CBAs include teacher-made tests based on daily instruction; chapter tests available from the publisher; work samples of paragraphs written by the student during class; math worksheets covering a specific objective based on the day's instruction; sight word lists used during reading instruction; and running records, including notes made by the teacher during oral reading (Layton & Lock, 2008). CBAs can also include direct assessments of academic skills through the use of probes, which are used to collect data on student performance. These probes are based on the books and materials used by the student. For example, in Mr. Harris and Ms. Butera's language arts class, a CBA in reading could involve each student orally reading short passages from the beginning, middle, and end of the reading basal to determine the suitability of the text to students' reading levels. Weekly spelling tests based on words studied during the week could comprise a spelling CBA, and authentic writing products, such as stories or paragraphs written by students, could be considered writing CBAs.

CBA Tips

Elementary and secondary content teachers can have students orally read selections from the textbook to determine the match between the readability level of the text and students' reading levels. Witt, Elliott, Kramer, and Gresham (1994) recommend the following:

- For each book in a basal reading series, select three 150- to 200-word passages (for first through third grades, use 50- to 100-word passages) one from the beginning, one from the middle, and one from the end of the text.
- Retype the passages on a separate sheet with corresponding running word counts in the right-hand margin.
- Selected passages should not have a lot of dialogue, should be text (not poetry or plays), and should not contain many unusual or foreign words.

- Make two copies of each selected passage. The child reads from one copy, and the teacher uses the other copy to mark student errors.
- Teachers who also want to assess comprehension can develop five to eight comprehension questions per passage to ask the student. These questions should include at least one who, what, where, why and inference question.
- The reading assessment is administered individually.
- Repetitions and student self-corrections made within three seconds are not counted as errors.
- Mispronunciations, substitutions, omissions, additions, and words not read within three seconds are counted as errors.
- The student's mean or median score on all three reading assessments can be used to determine the suitability of the text to the student's reading level. Generally, independent reading is associated with 98 percent accuracy, instructional with 95 percent accuracy, and frustrational with less than 90 percent accuracy. Therefore, a student who reads a 100-word passage with zero to two errors could read the text independently. Those who read with around five errors would be at their instructional level, which means they would need teacher support with the text. Those who read with ten or more errors would find the text too frustrating, even with teacher support.

Curriculum-Based Measurement

A cousin to CBA is curriculum-based measurement (CBM). CBM is a data collection system designed to provide teachers with quick, reliable information on student progress as well as the effects of their instruction (Layton & Lock, 2008). CBMs are considered to be valid, reliable alternatives to both standardized and teacher-made tests. In constructing a CBM, (1) skills are taken from the student's curriculum, (2) various forms of the assessment are administered repeatedly, and (3) the data inform teachers about how well students learned what was taught. Sampling skills from the curriculum helps teachers know if students are ready for new material or if they need additional review.

One type of CBM that provides data on students' reading skills is oral reading fluency (ORF). In administering ORF, the examiner presents the student with three passages of the difficulty expected for year-end competence, and the student reads each passage aloud for one minute. The score is the number of words read correctly. The median (exact middle) of the three passages is the recorded score.

When conducting oral reading fluency assessments, select passages containing at least 200 words, more depending upon the grade level. All passages used initially, as well as to monitor progress throughout the year, must be written at an equal level of readability, or reading difficulty.

Many teachers use passages designed specifically for repeated measurement, or CBM, rather than select passages from the textbook, as described earlier with CBA. Typically, passages from grade-level novels and textbooks are inconsistent in their reading levels, as they start several years above the assigned grade level and contain as much as a three-year range. Reading passages are available free online through the University of Oregon's Web site at http://dibels.uoregon.edu.

Other CBM sources for math, spelling, and writing are available for a fee. One such source is AIMSweb (https://aimsweb.com). In addition to providing CBM probes, these sites contain normative information and data management systems. A site license is needed to access all AIMSweb information except normative data. AIMSweb normative performance tables are calculated using the AIMSweb Pro Complete student database (www.aimsweb.com/products/systems/pro_complete/description.php). The information is presented by percentile rank and by fall, winter, and spring benchmark periods.

By using the CBA or CBM measures and the cloze passage procedures at the beginning of the school year, our co-teachers will have valuable information about their students. Data from these informal assessments enable co-teaching teams to determine if classroom materials are at the appropriate level for students.

Progress Monitoring

In addition to determining students' entry-level skills, CBMs can be used to monitor student progress in the grade-level curriculum. The initial CBM provides information about students' entry-level background knowledge and skills. Teachers can use an additional assessment tool, called progress monitoring, to assess how students are progressing within the curriculum. Progress monitoring allows teachers to use student performance data to evaluate continually the effectiveness of their instruction. Based on the results of the progress monitoring, teachers then adjust, modify, and change what they are doing to increase student learning. Student achievement increases when teachers use student progress monitoring (Safer & Fleischman, 2005).

Progress-monitoring CBMs are different from mastery tests. In mastery tests, the teacher tests for mastery of a certain concept being taught, such as double-digit addition with regrouping. After mastery is demonstrated, the teacher presents the next step in the curriculum. At different times during the year, different skills are assessed. In CBM testing, all the skills expected to be mastered by the end of the year are tested throughout the year. Each test is an alternative form with different test items but of equivalent difficulty. For example, in September, a CBM math test assesses all the computation, problem-solving, fractions, money, and geometry skills to be covered during the entire year, even though many of these concepts have not yet been taught. Student data from this assessment provides the baseline. Alternative, but equivalent, forms containing all the same concepts are administered in November, January, March, and May in exactly the same manner but with different items. Students' scores are analyzed to determine if their competency in the curriculum is increasing. If students are not showing growth, teachers provide additional instruction, a different curriculum, or a different instructional approach. In short, data from progress monitoring assessment inform instruction, because something in the teaching pattern must change if students are not advancing in the curriculum.

Teachers can design their own CBMs based on the material they expect students to have mastered by the end of the school year by following these steps:

1. Identify what curriculum material students are expected to master over the school year.

2. Using the identified material, create a number of probes, or short CBM tests.

3. Administer the probes at frequent intervals.

4. Use results to make instruction decisions, which may include the following:
    o Evaluating the appropriateness of curricular materials
    o Forming instructional groups
    o Identifying areas of difficulty that need intensive instruction

Progress-monitoring CBMs in math, reading, and writing are available from a variety of sources for a fee.

Pretests and Teacher-Made Tests

In addition to the CBA or CBM reading assessment, elementary and secondary teachers can develop a pretest to assess students' present levels of performance associated with the upcoming unit or topic. Students who display mastery on the pretest can be excused from completing many of the tasks associated with the unit. Instead, because they have tested out of the unit, they can contract for completing individual learning projects that extend their thinking and learning about the curriculum.

Some tips for developing a good teacher-made quiz include the following (Conderman & Koroglanian, 2002):

- For multiple-choice items, each question should be written in the form of a direct question (rather than an incomplete sentence stem). The question should be long enough and have sufficient detail to provide context for the answers, and responses should be written in about the same length and detail. Use "all of the above" and "none of the above" sparingly and do not offer tips to other test questions.
- For matching items, have a few extra answers that are not used (have extra distracters), place the longer phrases on the left column, and use matching items only for homogeneous items. In other words, do not mix names, places, and events in a matching section; use matching only for matching like items. Include no more than ten items in a matching section for students with disabilities.
- For true-false items, make sure only one concept is being assessed. Avoid taking sentences verbatim from the text, avoid taking an obviously true statement and inserting the word *not* to make the statement false, and avoid clue words such as *always, never, sometimes, often,* or *maybe.* Include an even number of true and false statements.
- For fill-in-the-blank items, place the blank at the end of the sentence, use the same-sized blanks, make sure the blank is an important concept, and make sure only one correct answer fills in the blank.
- For short-answer or essay items, provide some background or context for the writer, be specific in the question, suggest a length for the writer, and have a rubric or scoring guide developed ahead of time.

■ TEACHER BEHAVIORS

Regardless of the type of formative assessment being used, we offer these guidelines:

- Make sure students know the reason(s) for the assessment. Is this assessment used primarily for a grade? For self-assessment? For progress monitoring? To check understanding of a concept before introducing the next more complex concept? Sharing the reason(s) for the assessment may reduce pressure and instill motivation for students. Students may not realize that different assessments have different purposes. Similarly, parents appreciate knowing the different assessment purposes, so include this topic during teacher conferences and on your Web page.

- Chose the type of assessment based on the purpose. Short, frequent, informal teacher-developed assessments are typically used as formative assessments, while unit tests and state and district exams are used as summative assessments. Using group responses (see Chapter 7) is an efficient way to assess every student's skill level frequently. Typically, multiple-choice, matching, and true-false items assess recognition skills, while essay, short-answer, and fill-in-the-blank questions assess recall. Before designing the assessment, reflect on the objectives being assessed. Do students need to know a concept or apply it? Do they need to recognize a fact or recall it? What is the purpose of an essay—to assess writing skills, organization skills, abilities in applying a concept, or all of these? Lesson plan and course objectives, as well as state standards, provide an important frame of reference for aligning instruction, assessments, and standards.

- Use recommended practices for designing the assessment. Consider having a peer review the first draft of the assessment tool. Are directions clear? Have you eliminated tips that help students determine answers to any questions? Is the assessment easy to read? Do questions reflect recommended practices in their wording and format?

- For classroom assessments, ensure the assessment directly reflects your instructional emphasis and instructional sequence. For example, if you spent 50 percent of your unit on teaching about the food pyramid, then 50 percent of the assessment should be on the food pyramid. Similarly, questions on the assessment should be ordered to parallel the instructional sequence. The first few test questions should reflect what was taught during the beginning of the unit, for example. Ordering the assessment in this way parallels the way students have processed information from the instructional sequence.

- Ensure that students with disabilities, 504 plans, or other special needs receive their testing accommodations or modifications. Common testing accommodations include extra time, a reader, the use of assistive technologies, or even allowing students to use their notes. Some testing modifications include an adjusted grading system, a word bank, simplified wording, a different version of the test, testing only big ideas, and reducing the number of distracters in answers. These accommodations or modifications should be on student's IEP or 504 plan, and they should be frequently reviewed for their appropriateness.

- Use student student results on every assessment to improve instruction. Using student data in this way reflects the cyclical nature of the instructional-assessment process.

BACK TO OUR TEAM ■

Our co-teachers have been co-teaching for three years in a third-grade diverse language arts class, and now they serve as true team teachers. During their first semester of co-teaching, however, they spent a considerable amount of time discussing how they would use assessments to provide feedback to students and inform their instruction. Prior to co-teaching, Mr. Harris used standardized test scores to place students in reading and spelling groups. He determined report card grades based on student scores on weekly spelling tests, quizzes over stories in the basal reader, scores on workbook and worksheet activities, and writing accuracy skills as noted on student stories and other writing projects. He used more summative than formative assessments.

Open-Ended Questions

Ms. Butera had some thoughts about using more frequent and formative assessments. To understand Mr. Harris's current instructional and assessment practices, she decides to talk to her partner using open-ended questions. Open-ended questions are used to gather information. They are worded in ways that welcome honest responses. Their use, therefore, is very appropriate by co-teachers in the beginning stages of collaboration. To gather more information about the assessment practices, Ms. Butera could ask the following open-ended questions:

- What assessments do you typically use in language arts?
- How do you feel about those assessments?
- Could you tell me about challenges you have faced regarding these assessments?
- How do you grade students—including students with disabilities?
- If you could make any changes about the assessments you use, especially now that you have a co-teacher working with you, what changes would you make?
- I am curious about your thoughts on my role in assisting with assessment responsibilities.
- What else would you like me to know about your assessment practices?

Asking open-ended questions provides a safe way to initiate conversation due to their nonjudgmental approach. Asking the co-teacher's opinions and visions for working together validates that person's thoughts while opening an avenue for further discussion.

The Result

By asking open-ended questions, Ms. Butera got a better sense of Mr. Harris's challenges, vision, and needs. The questions also naturally led into a discussion of how Ms. Butera can meaningfully contribute to the vision.

By asking open-ended questions and sharing their thoughts, the co-teaching team establishes assessment goals for their class. They prioritized those needs as (1) determining students' entry skills, (2) using more frequent informal and formative assessments, and (3) re evaluating the ways in which students with disabilities are graded. They decided to begin by gathering authentic student data for grouping and diagnostic purposes rather than using state and district scores, incorporating more variety into their assessments by using formative assessments more frequently, and researching ideas on how to grade students with disabilities in inclusive settings.

The team plans for the first few days of their co-teaching experience. Rather than instructing students in the curriculum immediately, as had been practice, the team agrees to spend the first few days collecting student assessment data. For the first week, students will do some spelling, writing, and reading activities, which will provide valuable data for planning instruction and deciding on accommodations or modifications. Some assessments, such as the cloze reading and some writing and spelling activities, can be group administered, and Mr. Harris agrees to take the lead on those. Other assessments, such as the CBM in reading, need to be individually administered, and Ms. Butera will prepare, administer, and score these. For the most part, the teachers plan to use the one-teach, one observe model and the one-teach, one-drift model. The plan for the teachers' first few days together looks like this.

■ LESSON PLAN

Day 1

Both teachers introduce themselves as language arts teachers. The class develops classroom rules and expectations, and Mr. Harris explains that this week will be spent largely on finding out more about students through their reading, writing, and spelling. Ms. Butera explains that some activities will be done as a large group and others, such as some reading activities, will be done individually. Co-teachers do not use the word *test* or *assessment* as they share their weekly plan. For the first day, students complete their first structured writing activity, which is to write a good story using their choice of several story starters. Students are given 20 minutes to write.

Day 2

After reviewing expectations, Mr. Harris administers a large-group spelling pretest containing 50 randomly selected words from the district's third-grade spelling list. Results from this assessment will help the team determine spelling groups. Ms. Butera then administers the large-group-administered cloze reading assessment based on a passage from the middle of the basal reader. With the time remaining, some students begin their CBM reading assessment, while remaining students complete self-assessment and learning preference inventories, similar to those in Figure 8.3.

Day 3

All students begin by completing their second writing activity. Because this is a standard writing task, students are again given 20 minutes to write

Figure 8.3   Self-Assessment and Learning Preference Inventory

Name (first, last, and middle): _____

Birthday: _____ Age in years: _____

Three words that describe me are: _____

My best school subject is _____.

The class I need the most help in is _____.

In language arts, I am good at _____.

In language arts, I need to work on _____.

I learn best by _____.

The best way for me to study for a test is to _____.

I study best in an environment that is (quiet, a little noisy, or noisy).

I would rather do a project (by myself or with others) because _____

_____.

I like teachers who _____.

My goal in this class is to _____.

My goal this semester is to _____.

a good story based on a story starter. Then, Ms. Butera individually assesses students using the CBM reading. Mr. Harris has gathered some pencil-and-paper assessments on grammar skills and punctuation skills, which students also complete.

Day 4

As Ms. Butera works individually with students on the CBM reading assessment, Mr. Harris explains the language arts portfolio that all students will assemble throughout the semester. When students are not reading with Ms. Butera, they assemble their portfolios, decorate their portfolio covers, write letters to their parents about their portfolio, and place some items in their portfolios, such as their self-assessments and learning preference inventories. Mr. Harris has made copies of various graphs and charts that will be used throughout the year, which students also add to their portfolios.

Day 5

Students complete their third and final writing assessment using their choice of provided story starters. When students complete their story, Ms. Butera finishes working individually with remaining students on the CBM reading assessment. While she works individually with students in the hall, other students finish their portfolio assignment, and then Mr. Harris monitors students as they work in trios playing various language arts–related games. In preparation, Mr. Harris gathered board games like Scrabble Junior; computer games with a reading, spelling, or vocabulary theme; some hands-on activities with sentence strips; and so forth. As students complete their games and rotate through various stations, Mr. Harris observes students and makes notes of their behavior, skills, and enthusiasm for certain games over others. He quickly learns which students to separate and which activities are more appealing to the class.

■ ASSESSMENT RESULTS

Because DIBELS passages were available at their grade level and their district did not have a site license from AIMSWeb, the co-teachers decided to use DIBELS passages. One advantage of co-teaching is that while Ms. Butera assessed each student, Mr. Harris continued with remaining students. No instructional time was lost for this assessment procedure. Allowing for transition time, Ms. Butera was able to assess all students within three 45-minute class periods. During the transitions between students, she scored the three probes and determined the median ORF rate and accuracy for each student.

■ MANAGING AND ANALYZING DATA

Because her school did not have a site license for the data management system from either AIMSweb or DIBELS, Ms. Butera used the spreadsheet program on her computer to manage data. Although a bit more cumbersome and time consuming, the spreadsheet program is less expensive and a workable alternative for managing and analyzing student CBM ORF data.

The CBM data indicated that the majority of their students, almost two-thirds, were unable to read at a rate that would enable them easily to access material written at the third-grade level. The co-teaching team noticed a mismatch between students' reading skills and the readability of the third-grade book.

Similarly, results from the cloze assessment indicated that only two students achieved more than 60 percent on an upcoming story in the basal, which indicated that only these two students were at the independent level and could read the story without teacher assistance. Eleven students achieved scores between 40 and 59 percent, indicating they were at the instructional level and could read the story in class with teacher assistance. Eleven additional students achieved scores of less than 40 percent, which indicated frustration level.

This was an "a-ha" moment for Mr. Harris. In the past, he had assigned stories to be read independently along with worksheets and workbook pages. He prepared students for the story by activating student background knowledge, discussing the title, and helping students make predictions. He had assumed that the readability of all the stories in the third-grade basal were within the range of the majority of his students.

Through data from the ORF and cloze assessments, Mr. Harris realized that many other selections from the basal reader were probably out of the comfort zone of many students. Although this had been his impression, he now had supportive data.

As he changes the material he uses and his teaching techniques, Mr. Harris will need a way to ensure that students are learning. After obtaining baseline data on the reading skills of their students, our co-teaching team learned that many students were not reading with enough accuracy or fluency to access grade-level textbooks. While this information was helpful, it was not sufficient to monitor progress. The team also decided to conduct ORF progress monitoring and use frequent informal activities to ensure that students understand presented skills. If students do not improve at the expected rate, the team will need to examine their classroom instructional practices.

GRADING PRACTICES

These changes also prompted the team to discuss grading practices. Mr. Harris had used the same grading system and scale for all students prior to co-teaching. He had not thought about individualizing grading systems for students with disabilities. Discussing grading policies and practices early in the co-teaching relationship is an important proactive measure. Christiansen and Vogel (1998) recommend a decision model that includes these steps:

1. Determine district, state, and federal policies and guidelines regarding grading.
2. Identify your theoretical approaches to grading.
3. Identify your colleague's theoretical approaches to grading.
4. Cooperatively determine grading practices for individual students.

These authors also emphasize that effective grading policies must be consistent with school policies, meet the communication needs of the grading process, reflect the theoretical orientation of both teachers, and be consistent with the students' IEPs. Students with disabilities are entitled to special accommodations because of their special needs. Students in the K–12 public education system are not there just to be evaluated in relation to their peers. They are there to learn and be assessed on progress in a way that considers their disabilities. Sometimes teachers can and should grade students with disabilities like those without disabilities, but this practice should not be applied to all students (Friend, 2006).

Students with mild or high-incidence disabilities often are successful with appropriate accommodations, such as extra time for assignments or tests, an oral rather than a written response, tape-recorded materials and tests, and various assistive technologies. Accommodations do not change the standard, but they provide access for the student. Figure 8.4 provides additional examples of assessment accommodations. These should be agreed upon by the educational team.

Figure 8.4   Assessment Accommodations

A. Timing or Scheduling Accommodations

- Multiple testing sessions
- Testing sessions with specified time parameters and designated breaks
- Extended time to complete tests
- Untimed testing sessions
- Testing done at a time when the student is most likely to be successful

B. Setting Accommodations

- In a separate location with either a paraprofessional or teacher
- In a carrel
- Preferential seating within the classroom to reduce distractions
- In a comfortable location with minimal distractions

C. Presentation Accommodations

- Use a larger font or provide large-print editions of tests.
- Break work down into small segments but still expect all parts to be completed.
- Read directions aloud.
- Have the student repeat or paraphrase the directions to ensure understanding.
- Provide directions in small steps and in as few words as possible.
- Number and sequence steps in a task.
- Have the test given by a person familiar to student.
- Read the standard directions several times at start of exam.
- Reread directions for each new page of test items.
- Repeat directions as needed.
- Provide additional examples.
- Provide practice tests or examples before test is administered.
- Increase the space between test items.
- Group similar test items together.
- Place fewer items on each page.
- Enlarge the size of answer bubbles.
- Remind student to stay on task.
- Keep the number of items on desk limited.
- Use assistive technology (adaptive keyboard, word processor, voice-activated word processor, voice synthesizer, etc.).
- Provide student a place marker, special paper, graph paper, or writing template for maintaining position or improving attention.

D. Response Accommodations

- Allow student to mark answers in test booklet rather than on Scantron.
- Allow student to dictate answers to recorder.
- Allow student to audiotape responses.
- Provide periodic checks to ensure student is marking in correct spaces.
- Waive spelling, punctuation, and paragraphing requirements.
- Permit or encourage the use of a word processor or typewriter.

E. Material Accommodations (for Typical Course Assignments)

- Provide material with similar content but at an adjusted reading level.
- Provide books on audiotape.
- Provide chapter summaries.
- Provide peer readers.
- Provide completed study guide ahead of time.
- Provide page numbers to help student find answers.
- Allow two sets of textbooks, one at school and one at home.

Students with low-incidence disabilities often need accommodations and modifications in the general education classroom. Modifications are changes to the assignment or assessment, such as a different spelling list, a different math assignment, or a true-false exam rather than an essay exam. Some additional assessment modifications include rewording test questions, reducing the number of choices in a multiple-choice test, using a different grading scale such as pass-fail, using recognition tests rather than essays, providing a word bank or the first letter of the missing word in fill-in-the blank items, and shortening the test by focusing only on key concepts.

Similarly, some students may benefit from grading accommodations or modifications. These should be discussed at the IEP meeting and, as necessary, be approved by the administrator. Some school districts have policies about grading. Generally, report card grades based on accommodations do not require any special notation. However, report cards can include notations when grades are based on a significant change in the curriculum (Friend, 2006).

If IEP team members and school administrators agree that an individualized grading approach is needed, they may consider these possibilities: (1) awarding two grades: one for effort and one for work or one for work at grade level and one for work at the student's level, (2) grading based on progress toward the IEP, (3) using comments rather than a grade, (4) using general categories (S-U or Pass-Fail) rather than letter grades, (5) using personalized rubrics, (6) using a portfolio, or (7) using a combination of all of these.

After discussing the need for grading students based on their skill level, the co-teaching team realized that giving students with disabilities Ds in the general education classroom because their skills and performance were below grade level was inappropriate. Therefore, the team requested a meeting with the administrator to discuss appropriate grading alternatives that would accurately communicate students' progress in the curriculum.

ASSESSMENTS AND OTHER CO-TEACHING MODELS ■

During the first week together, the team primarily used the one-teach, one drift or the one-teach, one-observe model. Often, Mr. Harris coordinated large-group activities and assessments, while Ms. Butera conducted individual assessments with students in the hall. Other co-teaching models could be used in language arts, such as the following:

- *Station teaching:* Due to the variety of skills associated with language arts, station teaching can be used with students to review different reading, spelling, editing, speaking, and writing skills. Some station ideas include applying new editing or comprehension strategies, practicing spelling words in a game format, finishing a story by adding a creative ending, or making a book cover for a favorite book or story.

- *Alternate teaching:* Because the team is going to infuse more formative assessments into their teaching, they may want to use alternate teaching frequently. This model allows one teacher to review skills with individuals or small groups based on error analysis, while the other teacher leads instruction or other activities with the large group. The alternate co-teacher could help students edit their papers, reteach skills and concepts that students missed on practice sheets, introduce strategies, or reteach a concept using a different approach.
- *Team teaching:* With two teachers, students can be offered more choices for individual and group work, and objectives and assessments can be differentiated.

■ SUMMARY

This chapter emphasized the practice of using formative assessments. Frequent quizzes, probes, observations, and daily work are examples of formative assessments. These assessments provide immediate feedback to students regarding their progress while guiding teachers to decide whether to reteach, review, or advance to the next skill in the curriculum. The chapter also introduced the use of open-ended questions as a tool for gathering information from your co-teacher. Finally, the chapter emphasized the importance of providing assessment grading accommodations and, as necessary, modifications to students with disabilities and reporting grades in ways that respect both individual differences and the district's approved grading policies.

■ REFLECTIONS TO APPLICATION

As co-teachers, have we . . .

- Discussed the summative and formative assessments used in our class?
- Emphasized ongoing assessments to inform our instruction?
- Collected student data using a variety of techniques?
- Analyzed our textbook and other materials for readability?

■ ADDITIONAL RESOURCES

Books

Ainsworth, L., & Viegut, D. (2006). *Common formative assessments: How to connect standards-based instruction and assessment.* Thousand Oaks, CA: Corwin Press.

Benson, B., & Barnett, S. (2005). *Student-led conferencing using showcase portfolios* (2nd ed.). Thousand Oaks, CA: Corwin Press.

Flynn, L., & Flynn, E. (2004). *Teaching writing with rubrics: Practical strategies and lesson plans for grades 2–8.* Thousand Oaks, CA: Corwin Press.

Guskey, T. R., & Bailey, J. M. (2001). *Developing grading and reporting systems for student learning.* Thousand Oaks, CA: Corwin Press.

Hosp, M., & Hosp, J., & Howell, K. (2007). *The ABCs of CBM: A practical guide to curriculum-based measurement.* New York: Guilford Press.

McEwan, E. (2006). *How to survive and thrive in the first three weeks of school.* Thousand Oaks, CA: Corwin Press.

Munk, D. (2003). *Solving the grading puzzle for students with disabilities.* Whitefish Bay, WI: Knowledge by Design.

Quinlan, A. M. (2006). *A complete guide to rubrics: Assessment made easy for teachers, K–college.* Lanham, MD: Rowman & Littlefield Education.

Articles

Bradley, D. F., & Calvin, M. B. (1998). Grading modified assignments: Equity or compromise? *Teaching Exceptional Children, 21,* 24–29.

Goodrich, H. (1997). Understanding rubrics. *Educational Leadership, 54*(4), 14–17.

Jackson, C. W., & Larkin, M. (2002). Rubric: Teaching students to use grading rubrics. *Teaching Exceptional Children, 35*(1), 40–45.

McTighe, J., & O'Connor, K. (2005). Seven practices for effective learning. *Educational Leadership, 63*(3), 10–17.

Munk, D. D., & Bursuck, W. D. (2003). Grading students with disabilities. *Educational Leadership, 61*(2), 38–43.

Salend, S. J. (2005). Report card models that support communication and differentiation of instruction. *Teaching Exceptional Children, 37*(4), 28–35.

DVD/Video

Falvey, M. (Writer), & Fothergill, W. (Director). (1995). *Now we're including students, but how do we assess and grade them?* [DVD/VHS]. Greeley, CO: Team 6 Media Services.

Web Sites

4Teachers.org. (2008). *RubiStar: Create rubrics for your project-based learning activities.* Retrieved May 18, 2008, from http://rubistar.4teachers.org/index.php (RubiStar is a free tool to help teachers who want to use rubrics but do not have time to develop them from scratch.)

Discovery Education. (2007). *Discovery Education's Puzzlemaker.* Retrieved May 18, 2008, from http://puzzlemaker.discoveryeducation.com (Discovery Education has a worksheet generator that develops cloze activities and removes words randomly.)

9

Putting It All Together

Co-Teaching With Integrity

Eleventh-grade co-teachers Mr. Kibaki (general educator) and Ms. James (special educator) are reflecting on their first year of co-teaching. Mr. Kibaki has been teaching high school beginning, intermediate, and advanced algebra for five years. This was the first year of teaching for Ms. James. Co-teaching in math has become more prevalent in the Maple Tree School District due to the importance of student math scores on state and district tests and increased high school math requirements for all students. As this pair reflects on their co-teaching experience, they realize that they successfully addressed issues that potentially could have spelled disaster for them and their students. Although their personalities, instructional philosophies, and experience differ, the team navigated those differences with mutual respect and integrity. Further, even when differences occurred between them and on days when they felt lost, they kept their vision, which was on student achievement.

This team in a nutshell:

Grade level: 11

Classroom contextual factors: 32 students, 12 with IEPs or 504 plans

Co-teaching stage: Beginning

Interpersonal issue: Difference in style

Instructional challenge: Lack of parity in content area

WELCOME TO ALGEBRA 101   ■

Perhaps you can imagine Ms. James's reaction when she learned she would be co-teaching eleventh grade beginning algebra. Her initial thoughts: "I have not had a course in algebra in over ten years, and I don't know how to teach algebra." Although she knew about effective math instruction, nothing in her teacher preparation program had specifically covered teaching high school algebra.

Mr. Kibaki had been teaching his algebra classes on his own for five years. He loved his subject, and it showed. He was an engaging and effective teacher, and students liked him. Realizing that he was going to have more students with disabilities in his class made him a bit uncomfortable; his initial thoughts were: "I had one course in special education in my teacher preparation program. Will I need to redesign my entire curriculum that I have worked so hard at developing?" He was thankful to learn that the newly hired special educator would be co-teaching with him, but he wondered if co-teaching would really work.

This chapter summarizes one team's successful approach to co-teaching that resulted in high student achievement and collegial satisfaction on the part of both co-teachers. You will learn how the teachers respected each other's strengths and kept their focus on students. After reading this chapter, you will be able to do the following:

- List issues to discuss before co-teaching begins.
- Describe components of successful co-teaching.
- Describe methods for keeping co-teaching focused on helping students.
- Note the importance of personal integrity in co-teaching.
- Articulate the benefits of frequent reflection in co-teaching.

INITIAL MEETING   ■

As soon as Mr. Kibaki and Ms. James learned they would be co-teachers, they made a time to meet in Mr. Kibaki's math classroom. School would be starting in one week, and they did not have much time to plan, so both teachers did some preparation in advance of their initial meeting. Ms. James brought various communication and co-teaching checklists (see Chapter 1) and copies of articles about co-teaching, while Mr. Kibaki gathered much of his curriculum. *Each teacher anticipated the needs of his or her partner at this initial meeting.*

When Ms. James entered the math classroom, *she immediately felt welcomed.* Not only did Mr. Kibaki have student and teacher texts, test and quiz answer keys, and copies of previous lesson plans for the first few weeks of class, but he also greeted Ms. James with a warm smile and handshake. During this meeting, the team became acquainted and discovered some similarities and differences. Just from conversation, they discovered that Mr. Kibaki was outgoing, verbal, spontaneous, and witty and had a natural sense of humor, while Ms. James was serious, quiet, and deliberate and planned in her instructional approach. Even so, they *both shared a positive optimism* about working together and agreed to do some homework for their next meeting.

Specifically, both agreed to read the same articles on co-teaching, which would form their shared knowledge base. They also agreed to complete a self-inventory on their communication style (see Chapter 1), write "bulleted thoughts" about their learning and instruction philosophy and their algebra content knowledge, and list strengths they brought to the co-teaching endeavor. They used the co-teaching model from Chapter 1 as a basis for this "homework" assignment and agreed to respond to sentence stems like those in Figure 9.1. Additionally, Mr. Kibaki volunteered to ask the custodian to bring in a teacher's desk for Ms. James, and Ms. James agreed to read over the first chapter in the algebra text.

Figure 9.1   Initial Discussion Sentence Stems for Co-Teachers

1. I think the teacher's role is to _____.

2. Effective teachers _____.

3. I believe students should _____.

4. My ideal class would be _____.

5. Something that would embarrass me in class would be _____.

6. Some of my pet peeves include _____.

7. Some classroom rules I think are important include _____.

8. When students misbehave in class, _____.

9. I rate my knowledge and skills in this content area as _____.

10. Some strengths I bring to co-teaching include _____.

11. I feel supported when _____.

12. I am most nervous about _____.

■ PROACTIVE PLANNING

The team communicated several more times before students arrived. They shared responses from their sentence stems, which focused their discussion on the type of class they would be developing. *They also shared their needs as teachers as well as the needs of students.* For example, Ms. James indicated that she was nervous teaching large groups—especially in an unfamiliar content area. She also shared that she did not like being "put on the spot." She noted strengths in writing objectives, developing individualized behavior plans, analyzing student work samples for error patterns, developing creative review activities, and working with small groups. Mr. Kibaki indicated that he was not easily embarrassed, he could "go with the flow," his greatest class would be if all students were actively engaged, and he feared he might take over too much. His strengths were how much he cared about his students, content knowledge, rapport with students, various questioning techniques, and experience level. *Discussing each co-teacher's fears allowed the team members to avoid embarrassing each other, and articulating strengths helped shape future co-taught lesson plans.*

Mr. Kibaki also shared successful strategies based on his five years of teaching beginning algebra, such as (1) allowing time in class for students to begin homework, (2) assigning peer buddies who exchange phone numbers and e-mails, (3) placing homework reminders on the Web page, (4) allowing students to redo poorly completed assignments, (5) having a consistent classroom management system, (6) involving parents, and (7) having structure yet variety in class. In these early meetings, the team made sure they discussed their instructional philosophy and beliefs, what parity signals they would use to display equality, classroom routines, discipline, comfort with classroom noise, pet peeves, and how they would provide feedback to each other (Friend & Cook, 2007). The team made note of their differences in these areas so that each voice was heard. For example, Ms. James noted that she was more comfortable with a quiet classroom, while Mr. Kibaki liked a bit of productive classroom noise. *Jotting down these issues validated each person's opinion while providing a forum for discussing them during future planning and reflecting meetings.*

The team also looked at the co-teaching model (Chapter 1) and, throughout the year, discussed implications in each category. Some of the issues they faced and the ways they addressed them are included in Figure 9.2.

Throughout the course of the year, the team frequently revisited these concepts. Some specific ways they addressed these principles included the following:

- *Mr. Kibaki and Ms. James were vulnerable about their weaknesses.* Each partner had to admit what he or she did not know and articulate what made him or her uncomfortable in front of students. For example, although Mr. Kibaki enjoyed establishing a friendly, joking relationship with students and he did not mind being teased, he displayed a more serious communication style with Ms. James *because that fit her style.* Similarly, due to his experience, Mr. Kibaki did not require hours of planning time for each lesson, but he had to remember that the content was new for Ms. James and that she required advanced notification of changes in the lesson plan—especially when she was taking the lead instructional role.
- *Along with having her own copies of all materials, Ms. James also ordered supplemental algebra materials for herself and some students.* These supplemental materials were extremely beneficial when explaining concepts to students who needed a different approach. Some of these materials included: *Algebra* (Haenisch, 2004), *Discovering Algebra: An Investigative Approach* (Murdock, Kamischke, & Kamischke, 2002), *Hands-On Algebra* (Thompson, 1998), *Hands-On Equations*® (Borenson, 2007), and *Algebra Tiles Workbook* (Burgdorf & Robinette, 2002). Mr. Kibaki also found these materials helpful when he needed to provide a more hands-on or concrete approach. *Having a variety of materials available helped the team diversify instruction, group students, explain concepts in various ways, and individualize instruction.*

Figure 9.2   Learning Throughout the Year

Component	Issue	Addressed by:
Interpersonal Skills	Differences in interpersonal style	• Learn partner's communication style. • Respond to partner in ways commensurate with that style. • Frequently check to see if communication is working.
Content Knowledge	Lack of parity in algebra content	• Provide copies of core and supplementary materials for co-teacher. • Share lesson plans as much in advance as possible. • Answer co-teacher's questions with respect. • Allow co-teacher to contribute "behind the scenes," at least initially.
Teaching Behaviors	Engaging and spontaneous versus quiet and planned	• Recognize and appreciate different teaching styles. • Explain to students that different styles exist. • Allow beginning teachers to develop their own styles. • Remember that students can adapt to the teacher's style.
Philosophy of Teaching	Differences in role of teacher (e.g., facilitator versus dispenser of knowledge)	• Recognize that different teaching roles have their place. • Chose teacher role appropriate for lesson objective. • Allow each teacher to experiment with that teacher's role. • Use student assessment to help determine which role is/was most appropriate.
Co-Teaching Stage	Self-induced pressure to become successful team teachers quickly	• Start slowly and use "safe" co-teaching models. • Recognize co-teacher's strengths. • Avoid comparing your co-teaching experiences those of with others. • Develop your own measures of success.

• *The team started slowly and recognized each other's strengths immediately.* After analyzing student scores on an informal math pretest, for example, they noticed that some students did not have their basic multiplication facts memorized, while others were ready to begin the algebra experience. For the next few days, the team decided to group students based on pretest skills. Ms. James was comfortable teaching multiplication strategies to a small group of students, while Mr. Kibaki guided the remainder of the class in working on enrichment math skills.

Finally, the team specifically discussed how they would address co-teaching requisites of parity, shared resources, shared accountability, and mutual goals. *Throughout the year,* they met these in the following ways:

- *Parity:* Accomplished by including both names on all documents, door, board, and Web site; referring to each other as *Mr.* and *Ms.* in front of students; having classroom space and materials for both teachers; using terms such as *we* and *our;* acknowledging each person's strengths and skills; making decisions mutually rather than independently; ensuring that each teacher assumed "lead" and "support" instructional roles; sharing noninstructional tasks; and ensuring that both teachers taught *all* students.
- *Mutual respect:* Accomplished by maintaining confidentialities; addressing concerns with the co-teacher; using effective communication skills; and asking the partner their ideas and opinions.
- *Mutual goals:* Met by determining student goals for the week, keeping co-teaching "all about the kids," developing a shared vision about what successful co-teaching looks like, and frequently reflecting on co-teaching success.
- *Shared accountability for outcomes:* Noted by using *we* and *our* when referring to students, their progress, and the teachers' methods; sharing parent conferences and open house preparations; mutually determining student grades; and attending department, grade-level, IEP, and 504 meetings together.
- *Shared resources:* Evidenced by researching and sharing additional methods and materials, remaining open to teaching in different ways, and learning more about co-teaching.

INSTRUCTIONAL INTEGRITY ■

The team learned, discussed, and modeled effective math instruction by first reviewing math research from general and special education. Because their class included students with varying math abilities, they abandoned the one-size-fits-all instructional approach. Some students needed accommodations, such as multiplication cards, color coding, special seating, or cue cards with steps and examples; some needed modifications, such as alternative text and assignments; and some students did not require any curricular changes. The team made sure that students with IEPs and 504 plans received what they needed. They developed a chart, like the one shown in Figure 9.3, so they would remember each student's needs. They never embarrassed students about these adaptations. Toward the beginning of the semester, Ms. James led a class discussion and learning styles activity on the different ways students learn. She emphasized that all students have various strengths and needs and noted that some students need more assistance in algebra than others. Therefore, some students might be allowed to use a calculator or a multiplication table or be given extra time or reduced homework assignments, while others might not be allowed to use such supports. She discussed that *fairness* does not mean that every student in the class gets the same thing—instead, it means that all students get what they need.

Figure 9.3   Student Accommodations and Modification Chart

Student Name	Case Manager	Accommodations or Modifications

The team also used the following instructional principles whenever possible:

- *Teach or preteach vocabulary:* Students kept a math journal of terms and examples, which they referenced frequently. New terms were always pretaught, even if they appeared in bold in the textbook.
- *Teach for understanding:* Teachers presented new concepts using the concrete-representational-abstract sequence. In other words, they first demonstrated the concept (often with algebra tiles or other concrete objects). Then, they showed the same skill using pictorial representations, such as visuals, number lines, fraction bars, etc. Finally, they introduced the algebra symbols. The teachers also frequently asked "Why?" so students would not just memorize steps.
- *Connect to student's life:* The teachers became skilled at showing how many algebra principles could be connected to activities of daily life, such as cooking, sports scores, travel, shopping, and home repairs. They avoided phrases such as "You need to know this for the test," but instead found ways to make algebra relevant to students.
- *Use assessment data*: The teachers frequently assessed. They used scores from daily assignments, probes, short weekly quizzes, unit exams, and student discussion responses to pinpoint student errors. They used student errors as a guide for reteaching.
- *Introduce strategies and mnemonics:* Because many students had difficulty memorizing facts, equations, and properties, the class developed ways to remember these using teacher- and student-developed memory tricks.
- *Separate confusing elements:* The teachers previewed the curriculum and taught confusing elements separately. Sometimes this meant they deviated from the textbook sequence. They separated their instruction of terms, principles, or properties that were similar, that sounded similar, or that had confused students in the past.
- *Incorporate lots of review:* Almost every day, the team spent a few minutes reviewing with the class. They reviewed newly learned material, as well as material learned yesterday, last week, and two weeks ago. They developed various systems to use for review, such as board games, team games, or verbal reviews. Other days, they placed a few mixed problems on the overhead for students to complete as they walked in the door.

PERSONAL INTEGRITY ■

In addition to modeling effective instruction, the team made a commitment to exercise personal integrity. This was essential for maintaining the integrity of the team. Some guidelines forming their relationship included the following:

- *Anything that goes on in the math room, stays in the math room.* In other words, the team made a commitment to maintain confidentialities, bring concerns to the partner (rather than criticize the co-teacher behind her or his back), and never publicly say negative things about the class, the co-teacher, or the curriculum. When an issue arose, they first spoke to each other.

- *Do not bottle it up.* Rather than waiting until things were *really* bad, the team agreed that each of them would confront the other caringly if something was truly upsetting. However, they agreed to allow for some "grace" with the realization that no one is perfect and everyone makes mistakes. They agreed to bring the issue to the attention of the co-teacher face-to-face during their times of planning or reflection or via a phone call. Important issues, they agreed, would not be settled via e-mail due to its impersonal nature.

- *Do what you say you will do.* To work as a team, each teacher must follow through. The other teacher depends on you. Therefore, following through, respecting time lines, and being a person of action were critical principles for this team. If questions arose while preparing a lesson, if an emergency arose that might delay completion of a project, or if one teacher would be absent, the teachers alerted their partners as soon as possible.

- *Use effective communication skills.* The team worked diligently on communicating frequently and in a variety of ways, as well as using effective communication skills, such as actively listening when a partner had a concern, using *I* messages when sharing an issue, using open-ended questions when possible, and summarizing after a lengthy dialogue to check the accuracy of the message.

- *Handle conflict sensibly.* The team also realized that even with these proactive measures in place, conflict would occur due to the close and personal nature of co-teaching and the fact that conflict is natural in human interaction. Rather than avoid conflict, the team discussed how they would confront each other with important issues that concerned them. Mr. Kibaki wanted Ms. James to be direct with him. He shared, "Just tell me—I won't be mad." This was difficult for Ms. James, as her usual conflict style was to approach the person slowly and bring up the issue gradually. She agreed to be more direct in her style with Mr. Kibaki. Conversely, Ms. James requested a softer approach from Mr. Kibaki when he needed to share an issue with her. Respectfully, he agreed to do so. *In short, each teacher used an approach preferred—not necessarily by that teacher but by the co-teacher—when handling conflict.*

■ OTHER KEYS TO SUCCESS

When asked about what other factors led to the success of their co-teaching experience, Mr. Kibaki and Ms. James noted these additional components.

Parent Collaboration

The team agreed to emphasize positive interactions with parents. They made a "sunshine call" first when possible. This is a positive phone call alerting parents to improvement in their child, appropriate behavior, or other noteworthy accomplishments. For every five calls the team made to discuss a failing grade or a behavior issue, they made one call to a parent of a student who was making good progress. The team wanted to put students' performance in perspective. They made a commitment to contact each parent in writing, person, or by phone before Christmas.

Progress Reports

In an effort to be proactive, one of the co-teachers called parents before unsatisfactory midterm progress reports were mailed home. The calls offered more details about the reason for the progress report and welcomed parental ideas to address the issue. This was a huge success. No parent was shocked, and while other teachers received angry calls, Mr. Kibaki and Ms. James received none. These co-teachers were in control of the situation rather than on the defensive. They also sent home weekly reports printed from their grading program to students in the D or F range. When they sent these reports home to be signed and returned, they kept a copy for parent conferences. They also always called home before the report was sent. The team only had to do this once. After that, students did not try to hide the reports. As a result of these efforts, parents felt more involved and began working with their children.

Approach to Discipline

If a student broke a rule multiple times and other interventions had not been successful, one of the co-teachers took the student to the hall with the portable phone. While in the hall, the student called a parent or an adult in his life and told the adult what had occurred (e.g., disrupted class, forgot homework or materials). After that initial exchange, the co-teacher got on the phone to explain what the teachers were going to do. The parent and co-teacher then together decided the next steps. As a result of this approach, students seemed to make the connection when they disrupted the parent's and teachers' routine. This process was very effective and was rarely repeated.

Extra Tutoring and Help for Students

Sometimes co-teachers are tempted to keep the attention on their own needs. Clearly, if co-teachers are not getting along, students can feel the tension, and learning can be compromised. Although each teacher needs to be treated with dignity, respect, and sensitivity while experiencing equal ownership and investment in the class, co-teaching is really "all about the kids." Mr. Kibaki and Ms. James agreed that their co-teaching slogan would be "It's all about the kids." They even printed a banner, which was placed on their front wall, as their reminder and placed the motto on their Web site. They were committed to making their classroom a welcome community of learners with high expectations for appropriate behavior and academic skills. They wanted their actions to represent their belief that all students can learn.

The team felt some pressure to teach skills to mastery due to district test scores. To this end, they realized that they could not meet this goal by themselves just within the 50-minute algebra class. Early in the year, despite their best efforts, some students were in need of additional review and support. To keep the focus on students, both co-teachers made themselves available Tuesdays and Thursdays after school for one hour for open algebra tutoring. Because both co-teachers were available, students were divided into smaller groups and could receive the help they needed. When students had an upcoming test, the groups reviewed but differently than the way they did in class. This helped students who needed to review at a slower pace. Also, students tended to ask more questions in this safe setting. Some students attended the tutoring sessions to do homework, listen to music (which is played when one of the co-teachers is not teaching), or just chat. The co-teachers learned a lot about each student from this increasingly popular tutoring time. In addition to the afterschool tutorials, students were kept in at lunch for the first ten minutes if they had missing assignments or had to make up a test and could not stay after school. Students hated missing lunch, so this consequence reinforced the idea that they needed to do work at home and come to school ready to learn.

Common Planning

Every Wednesday, both teachers, in conjunction with another algebra teacher in the department, remained after school together to prepare lesson plans for the coming week. They used Figure 9.4 to guide their discussions. The initial plan was selected after reviewing the school district mathematics curriculum pacing guide and state standards. Each teacher had input at this stage. As the plan took shape, Ms. James focused on the specific needs of each student with an IEP and ensured that accommodations were being made. In addition, she created visuals to enhance instruction for each lesson. Ms. James took a copy of the plan and created an adapted plan, addressing any individual student needs by lesson. The team touched base during time before school to review the plan and make any last-minute adjustments. Even when one teacher was absent and a substitute was called, the substitute was expected to co-teach using the established plans.

Time for Reflection

Mr. Kibaki and Ms. James made a commitment to reflect on the co-teaching experience informally by addressing questions like those in Figure 9.5. Sometimes they found a moment to connect during class as students were working independently. Other times, they touched base after class, between periods while monitoring the halls, after school, and before leaving the building.

During their weekly common planning time, however, the team reflected more formally on activities relating to planning, instruction, and parent collaboration. They also discussed the co-teaching relationship and individual student needs. The team used Figure 9.6 to document their progress toward successful co-teaching with integrity.

■ SUMMARY

This chapter used a case study to articulate one team's successful approach to co-teaching that resulted in high student achievement and collegial satisfaction from both co-teachers. From the initial meeting to execution of

Figure 9.4   Co-Teacher Planning Form

General Educator: _____ Special Educator: _____

Subject: _____ Class Period: _____ Date of Lesson: _____

Lesson objectives:

Materials needed:

Lesson sequence:

<u>Co-Teacher</u>   <u>Instructional Responsibilities</u>

Assignment or independent practice:

Remediation needed:

Students who may need accommodations and modifications:

Figure 9.5   Sample Reflection Questions

1. What went well with our lessons today or this week?
2. Did we experience any surprises this week (pleasant or unpleasant)?
3. What do we need to work on—instructionally—for students?
4. Which students do we need to monitor, make contact with, or follow up with?
5. How did students do on assignments this week?
6. Based on student performance, do we need to review, or can we move forward in the curriculum?
7. Based on student performance, which students need more assistance?
8. What is our plan for the coming day days or week?
9. What is the most appropriate way to divide responsibilities for the upcoming day or days or week?
10. What do we need to work on—as co-teachers—to be effective?

lessons, methods were presented to keep co-teaching focused on helping students. The chapter showed how personal and instructional integrity were maintained through proactive practices, common planning time, parent collaboration, and student communication. This chapter also addressed the importance of frequent reflection in the co-teaching relationship.

◼ REFLECTIONS TO APPLICATION

As co-teachers, have we . . .

- Considered ways to share our instructional expertise?
- Shared our vision for the co-teaching experience?
- Committed ourselves to focusing on student needs?
- Communicated ways in which we will emphasize personal integrity?
- Scheduled a regular time to reflect on our co-teaching practices?

◼ ADDITIONAL RESOURCES

Books

Glanz, J. (2004). *Teaching 101: Classroom strategies for the beginning teacher.* Thousand Oaks, CA: Corwin Press.

Glasgow, N. A., & Hicks, C. D. (2003). *What successful teachers do: 91 research-based classroom strategies for new and veteran teachers.* Thousand Oaks, CA: Corwin Press.

Walker Tileson, D. (2005). *Ten best teaching practices: How brain research, learning styles, and standards define teaching competencies* (2nd ed.). Thousand Oaks, CA: Corwin Press.

Articles

Rockwell, S. (2007). Working smarter, not harder: Reaching the tough to teach. *Kappa Delta Pi Record, 44*(2), 56–61.

Figure 9.6 Co-Teaching With Integrity: Weekly Self-Evaluation Checklist

Date for Reviews: _____ Co-Teachers: _____

Planning	Yes/No	If No, Why?
Did we have scheduled time for coplanning this week?		
Did we both have input into the unit or lesson plan?		
Did we both readily accept each other's ideas?		
Are we both involved in planning for all students?		
Are these plans connected to standards and student outcomes?		
Are these plans submitted for administrative approval?		
Is our planning ongoing throughout the week?		
Instruction		
Did students hear from both of us?		
Did we present instruction in a variety of ways?		
Did we use research-based strategies?		
Did we both come in contact with all students?		
Did we both use inclusive language (*us, our, we*)?		
Relationship		
Did we set aside time to talk about our partnership?		
Did we amicably resolve issues related to our partnership?		
Parent Collaboration Issues		
Did we contact parents regarding grades this week?		
Did we contact parents regarding student behavior this week?		
Did we make one to five "sunshine" contacts this week?		
Did we ensure that the homework hotline Web site was updated this week?		
Student Issues		
Did we share updated grade reports with students this week?		
Did we invite students to attend homework club this week?		
Did we address concerns about specific students with administration, case managers, or support staff, if needed?		

References

■ PREFACE

Friend, M., & Cook, L. (2007). *Interactions: Collaboration skills for school professionals.* Boston: Pearson/Allyn & Bacon.

■ CHAPTER 1

Friend, M., & Cook, L. (2007). *Interactions: Collaboration skills for school professionals.* Boston: Pearson/Allyn & Bacon.

Gately, S. E., & Gately, F. J. (2001). Understanding co-teaching components. *Teaching Exceptional Children, 33*(4), 40–47.

Murawski, W. M., & Dieker, L. A. (2004). Tips and strategies for co-teaching at the secondary level. *Teaching Exceptional Children, 36*(5), 52–58.

Roy, P., & O'Brien, P. (1989, November). *Collaborative school: So what! Now what!* Paper presented at the annual meeting of the National Staff Development Council, Anaheim, CA.

Turnbull, A., Turnbull, R., & Wehmeyer, M. L. (2007). *Exceptional lives: Special education in today's schools* (5th ed.). Upper Saddle River, NJ: Merrill-Prentice Hall.

U.S. Department of Education. (2001). *To assure the free appropriate public education of all children with disabilities: Twenty-third report to Congress on the implementation of the Individuals with Disabilities Education Act.* Washington, DC: Author.

Villa, R. A., Thousand, J. S., & Nevin, A. I. (2004). *A guide to co-teaching: Practical tips for facilitating student learning.* Thousand Oaks, CA: Corwin Press.

■ CHAPTER 2

Friend, M., & Cook, L. (2007). *Interactions: Collaboration skills for school professionals.* Boston: Pearson/Allyn & Bacon.

Murawski, W. (2005). Addressing diverse needs through co-teaching: Take baby steps. *Kappa Delta Pi Record, 41*(2), 77–82.

Scruggs, T., Mastropieri, M., & McDuffie, K. (2007). Teaching in inclusive classrooms: A metasynthesis of qualitative research. *Exceptional Children, 73*(4), 392–416.

Sprick, R., Garrison, M., & Howard, L. (1998). *CHAMPS: A proactive and positive approach to classroom management.* Eugene, OR: Pacific Northwest Publishing.

■ CHAPTER 3

Coyne, M. D., Kame'enui, E., & Carnine, D. (2007). *Effective teaching strategies that accommodate diverse learners* (3rd ed.). Upper Saddle River, NJ. Merrill-Prentice Hall.

Dempster, F. (1993). Exposing our students to less should help them learn more. *Phi Delta Kappan,* 433–437.

Lenz, B. K., Schumaker, J. B., Deshler, D. D., & Bulgren, J. (1999). *The content enhancement series: The course organizer routine.* Lawrence, KS: Edge Enterprises.

Sorrick, M. (2007, Fall). *Understanding by Design.* Training presented in the Wheaton-Warrenville Community School District 200, Wheaton, Il.

Wiggins, G., & McTighe, J. (2005). *Understanding by design* (2nd ed.) Alexandria, VA: Association for Supervision and Curriculum Development.

CHAPTER 4 ■

Deshler, D., & Schumaker, J. (2006). *Teaching adolescents with disabilities: Accessing the general education curriculum.* Thousand Oaks, CA: Corwin Press.

Lloyd, J. W., Forness, S., & Kavale, K. (1998). Some methods are more effective than others. *Intervention in School and Clinic, 33*(4), 195–200.

Mastropieri, M., & Scruggs, T. (1998). Enhancing school success with mnemonic strategies. *Intervention in School and Clinic, 33*(4), 201–208.

Nagel, D., Schumaker, J., & Deshler, D. (1986). *The FIRST-letter mnemonic strategy.* Lawrence, KS: Edge Enterprises.

CHAPTER 5 ■

Carnine, D. W., Silbert, J., Kame'enui, E., & Tarver, S. (2004). *Direct instruction reading.* Upper Saddle River, NJ: Merrill-Prentice Hall.

Ellis, E., & Howard, P. (2007). Graphic organizers: Power tools for teaching. *Current Practice Alerts, 13.*

CHAPTER 6 ■

Birsh, J. R. (2005). *Multisensory teaching of basic language skills* (2nd ed.). Baltimore, MD: Paul H. Brookes.

Carnine, D. W., Silbert, J., Kame'enui, E., & Tarver, S. (2004). *Direct instruction reading.* Upper Saddle River, NJ: Merrill-Prentice Hall.

Ellis, E. S. (1989). A metacognitive intervention for increasing class participation. *Learning Disabilities Focus, 5*(1), 36–46.

Friend, M., & Bursuck, W. (2006). *Including students with special needs.* Boston: Allyn & Bacon.

Harris, K. R., & Graham, S. (1996). *Making the writing process work: Strategies for composition and self-regulation.* Cambridge, MA: Brookline Books.

Montague, M. (2006). Self-regulation strategies for better math performance in middle school. In M. Montague & A. K. Jitendra (Eds.), *Teaching mathematics to middle school students with learning disabilities* (pp. 89–107). New York: Guilford Press.

Morin, V. A., & Miller, S. P. (1998). Teaching multiplication to middle school students with mental retardation. *Education and Treatment of Children, 21,* 22–36.

Polloway, E. A., Patton, J. R., & Serna, L. (2005). *Strategies for teaching learners with special needs.* (8th ed.). Upper Saddle Back River, NJ: Merrill-Prentice Hall.

Sabornie, E., & deBettencourt, L. (2004). *Teaching students with mild and high-incidence disabilities at the secondary level* (2nd ed.). Upper Saddle River, NJ: Merrill-Prentice Hall.

Schumaker, J. B., Denton, P. H., & Deshler, D. (1984). *The paraphrasing strategy.* Lawrence: University of Kansas.

Schumaker, J. B., Nolan, S. M., & Deshler, D. (1985). *The error monitoring strategy.* Lawrence: University of Kansas.

Stein, N., Kinder, D., Silbert, J., & Carnine, D. (2006). *Designing effective mathematics instruction: A direct instruction approach* (4th ed.). Upper Saddle River, NJ: Merrill-Prentice Hall.

CHAPTER 7 ■

Feldman, K., & Denti, L. (2004). High-access instruction: Practical strategies to increase active learning in diverse classrooms. *Focus on Exceptional Children 36*(7), 1–12.

Klinger, J., Vaughn, S., Dimino, J., Schumm, J., & Bryant, D. (2001). *Collaborative strategic reading: Strategies for improving comprehension.* Longmont, CO: Sopris West.

Wilcox, T. (2003). *A screaming good time (WebQuest: A Middle School Graphing Adventure).* Retrieved March 1, 2008, from http://www.germantown.k12.wi.us/resource/coasterwq

■ CHAPTER 8

Albrecht, S. F., & Joles, C. (2003). Accountability and access to opportunity: Mutually exclusive tenets under a high-stakes testing mandate. *Preventing School Failure, 47*(2), 86–91.

Bangert-Drowns, R. L., Kulick, J. A., & Morgan, M. T. (1991). The instructional effect of feedback in test-like events. *Review of Educational Research, 61*(2), 213–238.

Black, P., & Wiliam, D. (1998). Assessment and classroom learning. *Assessment in Education, 5*(1), 7–74.

Christiansen, J., & Vogel, J. R. (1998). A decision model for grading students with disabilities. *Teaching Exceptional Children, 31*(2), 30–35.

Conderman, G., & Koroglanian, C. (2002). Writing test questions like a pro. *Intervention in School and Clinic, 38*(2), 83–87.

Friend, M. (2006, October). *Co-teaching: Addressing the challenges.* Paper presented at the 35th annual conference of the Learning Disabilities Association of Iowa, Des Moines.

Layton, C. A., & Lock, R. H. (2008). *Assessing students with special needs to produce quality outcomes.* Upper Saddle River, NJ: Merrill-Prentice Hall.

Safer, N., & Fleischman, S. (2005). Research matters: How student progress monitoring improves instruction. *Educational Leadership, 62*(5), 81–83.

Simpson, R. L., LaCava, P. G., & Sampson Graner, P. (2004). The No Child Left Behind Act: Challenges and implications for educators. *Intervention in School and Clinic, 40*(2), 67–75.

Vispoel, W. P., & Austin, J. R. (1995). Success and failure in junior high school: A critical incident approach to understanding students' attributional beliefs. *American Educational Research Journal, 32*(2), 377–412.

Weber, E. (1999). *Student assessment that works: A practical approach.* Boston: Allyn & Bacon.

Witt, J. C., Elliott, S. N., Kramer, J. J., & Gresham, F. M. (1994). *Assessment of children: Fundamental methods and practices.* Madison, WI: WCB Brown and Benchmark.

■ CHAPTER 9

Borenson, H. (2007). *Hands-On Equations®.* Retrieved May 18, 2008, from www.borenson.com

Burgdorf, R., & Robinette, M. (2002). *Algebra tiles workbook.* Vernon Hills, IL: Learning Resources.

Friend, M., & Cook, L. (2007). *Interactions: Collaborative skills for school professionals.* Boston: Pearson Education.

Haenisch, S. (2004). *Algebra.* Circle Pines, MN: American Guidance Service.

Murdock, J., Kamischke, E., & Kamischke, E. (2002). *Discovering algebra: An investigative approach.* Emeryville, CA: Key Curriculum Press.

Thompson, F. M. (1998). *Hands-on algebra: Ready-to-use games and activities for grades 7–12.* West Nyack, NY: Center for Applied Research in Education.

Index

CORWIN PRESS

The Corwin Press logo—a raven striding across an open book—represents the union of courage and learning. Corwin Press is committed to improving education for all learners by publishing books and other professional development resources for those serving the field of PreK–12 education. By providing practical, hands-on materials, Corwin Press continues to carry out the promise of its motto: **"Helping Educators Do Their Work Better."**